T0340155

The Cambridge Introduction to
Edward Said

One of the most famous literary critics of the twentieth century, Edward Said has been hugely influential far beyond academia. As a prominent advocate for the Palestinian cause and a noted music critic, Said redefined the role of the public intellectual. In his books, as scholarly as they are readable, he challenged conventional critical demarcations between disciplines. His major opus, *Orientalism*, is a key text in postcolonial studies that continues to influence as well as challenge scholars in the field. Conor McCarthy introduces the reader to Said's major works and examines how his work and life were intertwined. He explains recurring themes in Said's writings on literature and empire, on intellectuals and literary theory, on music and on the Israel/Palestine conflict. This concise, informative, and clearly written introduction for students beginning to study Said is ideally set up to explain the complexities of his work to new audiences.

Conor McCarthy is Lecturer in English at the National University of Ireland, Maynooth.

The Cambridge Introduction to
Edward Said

CONOR McCARTHY

National University of Ireland, Maynooth

CAMBRIDGE
UNIVERSITY PRESS

CAMBRIDGE
UNIVERSITY PRESS

University Printing House, Cambridge CB2 8BS, United Kingdom

One Liberty Plaza, 20th Floor, New York, NY 10006, USA

477 Williamstown Road, Port Melbourne, VIC 3207, Australia

4843/24, 2nd Floor, Ansari Road, Daryaganj, Delhi - 110002, India

79 Anson Road, #06-04/06, Singapore 079906

Cambridge University Press is part of the University of Cambridge.

It furthers the University's mission by disseminating knowledge in the pursuit of education, learning and research at the highest international levels of excellence.

www.cambridge.org
Information on this title: www.cambridge.org/9780521683050

First published 2010
Reprinted 2011

A catalogue record for this publication is available from the British Library

Library of Congress Cataloging in Publication data
McCarthy, Conor.
The Cambridge introduction to Edward Said / Conor McCarthy.
    p. cm.
Includes bibliographical references and index.
ISBN 978-0-521-86453-4 (hardback)
1. Said, Edward W. I. Title.
PN75.S25M33   2010
801'.95092 – dc22   2010015481

ISBN 978-0-521-86453-4 Hardback
ISBN 978-0-521-68305-0 Paperback

For Alice, Anna, Poppy, and William, and in memory of Rachel Corrie.

Contents

Acknowledgments

This book would not have been written without the support of many people. Firstly, my mother, though she is not here to read and question this book, always supported my projects and my interest in Edward Said.

My encounter with Edward Said began when Ellen Goodell gave me my first copy of *Orientalism*. I initially read Said with Seamus Deane, Thomas Docherty, and, in particular, Declan Kiberd, and for their guidance and encouragement I am very grateful. More recently I have learned much from conversations with Bashir Abu-Manneh, Joe Cleary, and David Lloyd.

I was fortunate enough to meet Edward Said on several occasions, and his brilliance, warmth, and openness were always compelling. Jean and Simone Mohr and Mariam Said have been very kind in facilitating the use of the cover photograph for this book.

I am grateful to Finbar Cullen at the Ireland Institute, to Ronit Lentin at Trinity College Dublin, and to my colleagues Joe Cleary and Colin Graham for opportunities to write and speak about Said. The library staff at the Mater Dei Institute of Education were very helpful to me. A most enjoyable residency at the Heinrich Boll Cottage, Achill, Co. Mayo, in July 2006 helped me get this work under way. Ruti Levi of *Ha'aretz*, and Nick Richardson of the *London Review of Books* assisted me with stray references.

It gives me particular pleasure to record that this work has been completed in the friendly and stimulating ambience of the Department of English at the National University of Ireland at Maynooth: my gratitude for their support and faith goes to Professor Christopher Morash and my colleagues in the Department, and also to Emeritus Professor Brian Cosgrove.

I owe a longtime debt to Norman Vance, for his erudition and example, and for his indefatigable support and kindness over many years.

It is to Ray Ryan that I owe the opportunity to write this book, and I am deeply grateful to him for that chance, and for his encouragement, cajoling, and endless patience during the process. Maartje Scheltens, Thomas O'Reilly, Caroline Howlett and Christina Sarigiannidou have been very tolerant and helpful in the production process.

My comrades Raymond Deane, Sally Eberhardt, Dara Fox, Andrew Kincaid, Chris Lee, Graham MacPhee, Mark Quigley, and Zohar Tirosh have provided me with an intellectual context of conversation and challenge. Luke Gibbons, Kevin Whelan, and the late Siobhan Kilfeather have all been generous to me over the years.

Thanks of a very special kind are due to Joanne Fox, for everything.

Chapter 1

Introduction, life, work

Beginning with Edward Said: history, biography, criticism *4*

Edward Wadie Said died at a hospital in New York City, on 25 September 2003, of complications attendant on the chronic form of lymphatic leukaemia with which he had struggled since 1991. He was sixty-seven years old. University Professor in the Department of English and Comparative Literature at New York's prestigious Columbia University, it can be reasonably speculated that he was at that time the most widely known intellectual in the world.

In the ensuing days, tributes to Said filled the media. United Nations Secretary-General Kofi Annan declared: 'Both the Middle East and the United States will be the poorer without his distinctive voice.'[1] Alan Brinkley, the Provost of Columbia University where Said had spent most of his professional career, said in *Columbia News* that 'Edward Said was a great scholar, a great teacher, and a beloved member of the Columbia community for 40 years.' Furthermore, Brinkley said, 'We will greatly miss this kind, gentle, and generous colleague and friend. It is hard to imagine Columbia without him.' Meanwhile, Columbia's President, Lee C. Bollinger, opined that Said's 'death is an irreplaceable loss to the realm of ideas and for those who believe in the redemptive power of the life of the mind'.[2]

Others remembered Said differently. 'A mighty and a passionate heart has ceased to beat', Alexander Cockburn, the radical Anglo-Irish journalist and leading figure of the New Left, wrote on his *Counterpunch* website. Cockburn suggested that: '[A]t the top of his form his prose has the pitiless, relentless clarity of Swift', a compliment Said would have enjoyed, and a hint at his reputation as a polemical writer, as a writer 'to the moment', responding with wit and learning to current events.[3] But this was also an indication of Said's controversial status, a matter that emerged in other obituaries.

The *New York Times* notice, by Richard Bernstein, was notable in this regard. It was preoccupied with Said's Palestinian nationalism, making cursory and inaccurate remarks about his literary-critical works. It suggested that Said's first book, *Joseph Conrad and the Fiction of Autobiography* (1966), was where 'he began to explore themes that led to his theories about culture and imperialism', yet what is striking about this book is its largely apolitical understanding of Conrad. Empire would not become a major theme of Said's criticism for another decade. Bernstein suggested that in *Culture and Imperialism* (1993), Said portrayed E. M. Forster, Conrad, and Rudyard Kipling as having been 'engaged in a novelistic process whose main purpose was not to raise more questions . . . but to keep the empire more or less in place', yet in this book Said goes to considerable lengths to show how anxiety about the future of empire is dramatised in such works. Of Said's most famous book, *Orientalism* (1978), Bernstein argued that it was a relativistic work that denied the possibility of 'objective neutral scholarship on Asia and especially on the Arab world'. He cited only negative assessments of the book, such as that of the English historian J. H. Plumb, without exploring the massive influence the book has had on a wide variety of humanistic and social-scientific fields.

More aggressively, the obituary concentrated on Said's Palestinian politics, and linked him to positions that he never took up when alive. It noted that Said was for fourteen years a member of the Palestine National Council, the Palestinian parliament-in-exile, while also pointing out that George Habash, leader of the Popular Front for the Liberation of Palestine, sat in the same assembly. Even more pointedly, Bernstein associated Said with Abu Abbas, 'a member of the PLO executive committee who is believed responsible for the hijacking of the Italian cruise ship *Achille Lauro* and the murder of an American tourist, Leon Klinghoffer, who was in a wheelchair'. Said's condemnation of Abbas as 'a degenerate' was, for Bernstein, clearly fatally eroded by Said's alleged description of Israeli former Prime Ministers Menachem Begin and Yitzhak Shamir as terrorists also. Said was referring to Begin's and Shamir's leadership of the Irgun Zvai Leumi and the LEHI groups of far-rightwing Jewish guerillas in 1940s Palestine. Bernstein noted Said's criticism of Ayatollah Khomeini's fatwa on Salman Rushdie and his description of Saddam Hussein as 'an appalling and dreadful despot', but reckoned that Said 'was far more critical of the West and of Israel and their approach to the Arab world than he was of the Arabs or their leaders'.[4]

The *New York Times* a few days later published a 'correction' to its original obituary. The original had 'misidentified the city that was [Said's] childhood home'. Said was born in Jerusalem in 1935, the article acknowledged, but 'his family's home was Cairo; they did not move from Jerusalem'. This adjustment was an echo of the attack by Justus Reid Weiner, in *Commentary*, an American Zionist magazine, on Said's patrimony in 1999, just as he published his memoir *Out of Place*. Weiner suggested that Said had invented a mythical childhood in Palestine, yet had been a scion of a wealthy Cairo family.[5]

Other writers noted the sourness of the *New York Times* article. Michael Wood, in the *London Review of Books*, argued that the *Times* obituary 'was full of apologies for being there at all – as if merely to mention Edward's name was to be a partisan'.[6] Marina Warner, in *Open Democracy*, suggested that it 'disgracefully rehearses ancient grudges and slurs, not recognising that the secular polity Edward so fearlessly and honestly struggled for in Israel/Palestine resembles the life of its own polyglot and multiethnic Manhattan rather more closely than Sharon's Israel'. The *Times*, for Warner, in Said's home town of forty years, 'managed to be mean-spirited about one of the finest representatives of some ideals of the old United States . . . : freedom of speech, independence of mind, civil conscience and humanist sympathies across all borders of ethnic and political identity'.[7]

The point here is not merely to enumerate the obsequies paid to Edward Said – evidently a major task in itself – but to show how even in death Said's reputation and work polarised and polarises opinion. In principle at least, Said would have welcomed this ferment of interest – not merely the adulation, but also the contrary opinions. Much of the power and interest of Said's literary-critical and political work was derived from his sense of writing as a practice and cultural form taking active part in its circumstances, in day-to-day social and political debates, movements, and struggles. Said's favoured term for this idea, as we shall see later in this book, was 'worldliness'.

Why was Said so controversial? We can start by saying that he was controversial on at least two levels. Academically, he was controversial because his work crossed disciplinary boundaries, 'interfering' (a term he on at least one occasion raised to a description of right intellectual practice) in areas outside of his professional expertise; and because he engaged frequently in an historicist criticism that sought to locate works of Western literature in the context of empire.[8] Outside the academy, Said was controversial because he was active in the cause of Palestine, the place of his birth and patrimony. Much of Said's published work was actually on the 'question of Palestine', a fact not always attended to in assessments of his work, and there is a strong case to be made that his interest in Palestine significantly influenced his entire *oeuvre*.

This book seeks to perform a number of tasks. It will introduce Said by way of a brief discussion of his memoir of his early life, *Out of Place*. It will then offer an account of Said's major works and projects, by moving into his writings along two trajectories. Firstly, it will explore Said's work through his major influences and intellectual contexts. Secondly, it will explore the same work as it is presented and organised in his most important books. Lastly, the book will give a brief account of some of the chief responses to Said's work.

This description seems cut and dried, as if these areas could be easily divided and held apart. What the reader will realise fairly quickly is that these areas actually routinely and importantly intersect in Said. The life will illustrate and inform our understanding of the work, and the work will be revealed as part of Said's way of living his life. The influences on him will be revealed to have been both reproduced and re-inflected in new ways. Equally, Said will be shown often to have responded in a dynamic manner to receptions of his own work.

At a conference to commemorate Said and his work held at the School of African and Oriental Studies at the University of London in 2004, the British Jamaican sociologist Stuart Hall finished his talk by saying of Said that 'we will not see his like again'. In this formulation, Hall was pointing out both Said's evident importance for the academic humanities and for the Palestinian cause, and also, in a less banal way, the fact that a very particular complex of historical, political, cultural, and intellectual forces combined themselves in Said's life and work.[9] The conditions of possibility for a figure of Said's ilk are passing, Hall was suggesting. This is a valuable point, as it allows us to start thinking historically about Edward Said. Let us look briefly both at the history from which Said himself emerged and, in a preliminary way, at how Said thought about the self and history, at the start and the end of his career.

Beginning with Edward Said: history, biography, criticism

Edward Said was born in 1935, to Palestinian parents, in a large stone house in Talbiyah, in the western quarter of Jerusalem. His father, Wadie Said, was a successful Palestinian businessman, whose stationery firm was headquartered in Cairo. The Said family moved in this period in a circuit between Jerusalem, Cairo, and the Lebanese hill resort of Dhour el-Shweir. Edward was educated at various schools in Jerusalem and in Cairo, culminating in his time spent at Victoria College, a prestigious school run by British teachers for the Arab elite.

In his early teens, Said was expelled from Victoria College, and his parents took the drastic measure of sending him to the United States, to Mount Hermon, a preparatory school in New Hampshire. From there, the young Said moved on to Princeton, and eventually to Harvard for graduate study. In 1963, he became an assistant professor at Columbia University in New York City. He won tenure in 1966, and spent the rest of his professional life there.

Even from this very basic sketch, then, it is possible to see that Edward Said, the prominent Palestinian American literary critic and public intellectual, emerged out of a complex network or conjuncture of historical, ethnic, and political forces. It is fair to say that these forces shaped him, but it is also important to note that without this context or set of contexts, the extraordinary phenomenon that was 'Edward Said' would not have had the same importance or force.

By the time Said was born, the forces that would shape the modern Middle East about which he was to write so often were already crystallising, in the form of extensive Jewish immigration to Palestine and emergent Palestinian national consciousness, which would lead eventually to partition, war, and the ethnic cleansing of approximately three-quarters of a million native Palestinians as a result of the bloody birth of Israel in 1948. This historical background is important to Said's work, in ways that are sometimes explicit, as in his critical and political writing on Palestine and on the Middle East more broadly, and also equally often implicit. In an interview with the editors of the avant-garde critical journal *Diacritics*, on the occasion of the publication of his first major book, *Beginnings* (1975), Said declared that:

> until fairly recently I led two quite separate lives, which has always made me acutely appreciative of Conrad's *The Secret Sharer*. On the one hand, I am a literary scholar, critic and teacher, I lead a pretty uncontroversial life in a big university, and I've done a fair amount of work which has always been plugged into the established channels. That's a function of a certain education, the appearance of a certain social background. Yet I lead another life, which most other literary people say nothing about (and this is a kind of acrobatics which people who know me can manage, with my helping them along: I've been very good at this). It's as if it isn't there, although many of them know that it is. My whole background in the Middle East, my frequent and sometimes protracted visits there, my political involvement: all this exists in a totally different box from the one out of which I pop as a literary critic, professor etc. Now the second, and older, life is encroaching fairly seriously on the other one, and this is a difficult juncture for me.[10]

This interview took place just at the point when Said was about to begin what might be called the major phase of his work. He had just published *Beginnings: Intention and Method*; he had already written most of the book that was to make him internationally famous, *Orientalism*; he was already at work on *The Question of Palestine* (1979); and he was also at this time writing and publishing many of the essays that would make up *The World, the Text, and the Critic* (1983). It is significant that it is precisely at this moment that we find Said reflecting on his complex identity as an advanced Euro-American critic with a Palestinian background, and striving to bring each of these spheres to bear on the other. It is a truism to say that much literary criticism is a form of sublimated or hidden autobiography, but with Edward Said we will find that the links between national history and critical work have an unusual salience.

Modern critics debate the distinctions between 'memoir' and 'autobiography'. It is suggested that autobiography makes a claim to comprehensiveness, objectivity, and accuracy, while memoir is more modest, self-consciously impressionistic, without aspiration to rigour or historical status. Said describes his book as 'a memoir', and he opens its Preface with a statement of its conditions of production and of its justification:

> *Out of Place* is a record of an essentially lost or forgotten world. Several years ago, I received what seemed to be a fatal medical diagnosis, and it therefore struck me as important to leave behind a subjective account of the life I lived in the Arab world, where I was born and spent my formative years, and in the United States, where I went to school, college and university. Many of the places and people I recall here no longer exist, though I found myself frequently amazed at how much I carried of them inside me in often minute, even startlingly concrete, detail.[11]

Furthermore, he believes that the book has

> some validity as an unofficial personal record [of the years between his birth and the completion of his doctorate in 1962]. I found myself telling the story of my life against the background of World War II, the loss of Palestine and the establishment of Israel, the end of the Egyptian monarchy, the Nasser years, the 1967 War, the emergence of the Palestinian movement, the Lebanese Civil War, and the Oslo peace process. These are in my memoir only allusively, even though their fugitive presence can be seen here and there.[12]

We can take from this the point that Said believes that his narrative of his youth has a significance beyond the personal. His story can be read in a number of ways. Schematically, we might say that these are: (1) the personal level – the description of Said's childhood in Jerusalem, Cairo, Lebanon, and the United States; (2) the level of historical reconstruction or recovery – Said is clearly interested in his story's status as 'a record of an essentially lost or forgotten world', and in its ability to reinstall and give voice to that world; (3) the political-historical level – Said's life intersects with and illustrates the turbulent and varied history of the Middle East since the 1940s.

In using Said's memoir, and his other autobiographical writings, we must bear a number of theoretical points in mind. Principally, most of these writings date from late in his life. This means, naturally, that he writes of his life with the benefit of hindsight, and with the intellectual equipment of a lifetime's work in literary study. Said was not just any memoirist when he came to write this work: he was one of the most prominent literary critics in the world. It is inevitable, therefore, that the ideas, skills, and techniques of his training and years of study would affect his writing about his own past.

For the fact is that *Out of Place* is configured in ways that conform to a number of Said's critical and intellectual preoccupations through his career. Said himself makes this very clear in 'Between Worlds', an essay he published while writing the memoir.[13] He begins this essay by remembering that his first book was on Conrad – *Joseph Conrad and the Fiction of Autobiography* – and by noting Conrad's status as 'the wanderer who becomes an accomplished writer in an acquired language, but [who] can never shake off his sense of alienation from his new – that is, acquired – and . . . admired home'.[14] For Said, Conrad was the writer of 'dislocation, instability and strangeness' *par excellence*: 'No one could represent the fate of lostness and disorientation better than he did, and no one was more ironic about the effort of trying to replace that condition with new arrangements and accommodations.'[15] Marlow, Conrad's famous narrator, enters the 'heart of darkness' only to find that Kurtz was there before him, and that he nevertheless cannot tell the whole truth. Said attributes both this quest for truth, in Conrad, and the ironic suspension of its success, to Conrad's exile from his Polish background. 'Eventually', he writes, 'we realise that the work is actually constituted by the experience of exile or alienation that cannot ever be rectified.' Said finds this dilemma most pointedly dramatised in Conrad's short story 'Amy Foster', where the exiled young man washed up on England's shore finally dies 'inconsolable, alone, talking away in a language no one could understand'. For Said, this image, which he had also mobilised in a much earlier essay 'Reflections on Exile', is the ultimate representation of the pain of exile. He suggests that Conrad himself, the Polish exile, must have feared such an end.

But as the Irish critic Seamus Deane suggests in a fine essay on *Out of Place*, this is clearly Said also writing about himself.[16] As Said himself says, Conrad has run through his writing 'like a *cantus firmus*, a steady groundbass to much that I have experienced'.[17] In the most literal sense, we find Conrad as the subject of Said's doctoral dissertation and of his first book based on that dissertation. His work is treated at length in *Beginnings*, Said's first major theoretical statement, published in 1975. It also appears in *The World, the Text, and the Critic*, published in 1983, and then again in *Culture and Imperialism* (1993). Said wrote more about Conrad than he did about any other single figure. Clearly, he had made a series of powerful identifications with the Polish writer. We may then think of Said's life and career as an effort also to evade the fate of Yanko Goorall, the young hero of 'Amy Foster', and indeed to avoid the fate of numerous other Conradian heroes, Marlow most notably, for whom communication is always fraught and frequently a failure. For Conrad, and for Said, we may take it that writing emerges out of an existential fear of silence.

Describing the way he came to write the memoir, Said tells of how he had learned in 1991 of his diagnosis with the leukaemia that would eventually kill him, and this prompted him to try to put narrative order on his life. 'I found myself brought up short with some though not a great deal of time available to survey a life whose eccentricities I had accepted like so many facts of nature.' In this attempt, 'I recognised that Conrad had been there before me.'[18] Yet Said sees that the moves that Conrad made, away from his Polish patrimony, and towards Englishness (initially via the medium of the French language), were in many ways not as wrenching as those that he himself had made, from Palestine and Egypt, to the United States and American academia.

But Conrad is only the most explicitly acknowledged influence here. As we shall see in Chapter Two, Said early in his academic career conceived a fascination with the eighteenth-century Italian philosopher Giambattista Vico. At the moment when he published his study of Conrad, Said also published an essay entitled 'Vico: Autodidact and Humanist'. Vico took himself and his own life, and his own intellectual leanings, as the start of his project:

> For he was preeminently an autodidact (*autodidascolo*) . . . Everything he learned, he learned for and by himself; he seems to have been convinced of his individuality and strength of mind from his earliest days, and most of the time his *Autobiography* is an account of this self-learning.[19]

Preparing to read Vico's philosophical masterpiece, *The New Science*, in relation to Vico's *Autobiography*, Said points out that what he believes to be 'the anchoring centre of Vico's work . . . is a paradigm of the disengaged, neutralized mind that is locked in a conflict with itself. The mind's role as an infinite series of modifications on the one hand is opposed by its role on the other as total structure.'[20] It is important for us to realise here, with our brief discussion of Said's early life and his writing about that early life in relation to Conrad, that this model of intellectual activity and linguistic, social, and historical analysis as evolving out of an internal mental drama is one which Said held over the course of his long and varied career. Writing a memoir was entirely of a piece with that model of work, and that sense of thought as both dramatic and conflictual. Writing a memoir was, in terms that Said had set out himself at the start of his intellectual career, a highly Vichian activity. Writing a memoir was, at least in part, Said turning back to reflect – in terms that would echo through his writings – on his own 'autodidacticism', his own 'self-learning', his own 'beginnings', his own 'authority' as an author.

One of the first and perhaps most important things to note about *Out of Place* is that it is a narrative not only about growing up in Jerusalem, Dhour el-Shweir, and Cairo, but also about moving into the West, towards the United States. *Out of Place* concludes with Said as a graduate student at Harvard, about to take up employment at Columbia University in New York City, where he spent the great bulk of his professional life. To this extent, then, the comparison with Conrad, who identified ever more powerfully with England as his life and career developed, holds. But while Jozef Teodor Nalecz Korzeniowski became Joseph Conrad, and was offered a knighthood (though he turned it down), Edward Said never became fully or comfortably American. The Scottish historian of nationalism, Tom Nairn, wrote in 1994 of Said that he was marked as a member of a Third World elite destined for successful Western metropolitan assimilation, yet he had, over his career, turned back to his natal place and tried to do justice to its politics. The effort, Nairn suggests, broke Said apart.[21] Yet, what we find in 'Between Worlds' is Said reveling in this status.

In the opening chapter of the memoir, Said discusses his name. In his name, he finds an opening formulation of the paradoxes of identity that shaped his life, and also his work. All families invent their parents and their children, he points out, but he finds that there was always something anomalous about the way that he was invented: 'Yet the overriding sensation I had was of always being out of place.'[22] Thus, in his first sentence, Said is acknowledging that his family shaped him, but also, implicitly, that he is now engaged in the act of giving an 'invented' shape to his family. For Said, the primary paradox of his identity is to be found in the oxymoron or contradiction of his own name: '"Edward", a foolishly English name, yoked forcibly to the unmistakably Arabic family name Said'.[23] Edward, his mother told him, was the name of the English Prince of Wales in 1935, the year of Said's birth. He describes how in later years he would, depending on the social situation, stress either his English name, or his Arabic one. He always resented and was unsettled by the unbelieving reactions of acquaintances and friends: 'Edward? Said?' The conjoining of as quintessentially English a name as that borne by the Prince of Wales, and an almost stereotypically Arab name, is suggestive of the unresolved paradoxes of his identity.

If this name was peculiar and somewhat confusing for a child and young man, its contradictions and discomforts did not ease or go away. Rather, as Said tells his readers more about his family background, the jarring ambiguities only increase and become more glaring. He tells us that he could not find any Said grandparents. He cannot remember which was his first language, Arabic or English, but 'the two have always been together in my life, one resonating in the other, sometimes ironically, sometimes nostalgically, most often each correcting, and commenting on, the other'.[24] This he attributes to the influence of his mother, who spoke to him in both languages, though she always wrote to him in English. But she also deployed the two languages in different ways: Arabic – 'forgiving and musical' – for love and intimacy with her young son, English – 'more objective and serious' – for discipline and order.[25]

Hilda Said's background was complex and confusing; that of Said's father, Wadie, was even more so. She was born in Nazareth, to a Palestinian father and a Lebanese mother. She was schooled in Beirut. Even her father's career hints at the geographical variousness that would be part of Edward's life – he was the Baptist minister in Nazareth, though he was originally from Safad, 'via a sojourn in Texas'.[26] Wadie Said was an American citizen, but even his name is a matter of confusion: his surname had been Ibrahim, and later in his life he changed Wadie to William: 'I still do not know where "Said" came from, and no-one seems able to explain it.'[27] Said tells us that his father had been encouraged by his family in 1911 to evade being drafted into the Ottoman Turkish army by escaping to the United States. Said compares the laconic and sketchy manner in which his father told him of his journey to America to the stories of Horatio Alger. Wadie travelled first to Liverpool, in his late teens, and then worked his passage to New York as a waiter on a transatlantic liner. In America, he became a salesman, and went to university. He served with the American Expeditionary Force in France in 1917, acquired American citizenship, and set up a painting company in Cleveland. He returned to Palestine in 1920, apparently at his mother's suggestion, as William A. Said: he had 'quite abruptly turned sober pioneer, hardworking and successful businessman, and Protestant, a resident first of Jerusalem then of Cairo. This was the man I knew.'[28]

Said sets up a dramatic contrast between his parents. His father is represented as a formidable Victorian patriarch – energetic, driven, and commanding: 'a devastating combination of power and authority, rationalistic discipline, and repressed emotions'.[29] Wadie Said's control of his son is described as a 'regime' that has induced in Edward a relentless and unsettled sense of never having achieved enough, the necessity of '"never giving up"'. Hilda Said, in comparison, was 'certainly my closest and most intimate companion for the first twenty-five years of my life'.[30] He attributes to her influence certain crucial traits he sees in himself: chronic sleeplessness, worry about alternative paths of action, restless energy, his interest in music and language, and also in style, and a combination of both sociability and 'a cultivation of loneliness as a form both of freedom and of affliction'.[31] But there was also a less happy side to his relationship with his mother: his sense that she would sometimes, inexplicably, withdraw her affection or attention from him. This added to his sense of loneliness, and his sense of shifting between different emotional conditions: 'Between my mother's empowering sunlike smile and her cold scowl or her sustained frowning dismissiveness, I existed as a child both fortunate and hopelessly miserable, neither completely one nor the other.'[32]

So the young Edward grew up, 'sliding' between his relationship with his father and that with his mother, turning to each of them for different things, striving endlessly to please them in their respective ways. 'I called my father Daddy until his dying day, but I always sensed in the phrase how contingent it was, how potentially improper it was to think of myself as his son.'[33] His self was therefore perpetually not itself, ill at ease, always living in the present tense, never able to relax or be at home. This sense of self-division that Said describes led to his having the odd sense of frequently observing 'Edward', himself, at a certain remove. So he was, as he says, the construct of his parents, a construction necessitated by the patent self-invention of his parents themselves. Furthermore, this constructed 'Edward' was worked up out of a rag-bag of unsorted materials: his Protestant Palestinian parents, members of a minority religion (Episcopalian Protestantism) and of a minority ethnicity in British-ruled Cairo; American influences from Wadie's time in the United States; broken and scattered schooling, including British colonial education. Inevitably, the Said family, and young Edward himself, were, to paraphrase the German poet Rainer Maria Rilke, 'beginners in their circumstances', always making themselves over and anew: 'Could "Edward's" position ever be anything but out of place?'[34]

Thus, even merely in the opening chapter of his memoir, Said sets the scene for an unsettled childhood, but also for a beginning strikingly in accordance with his later acquired intellectual principles. Young Edward understands himself as split between 'Edward', a simulacrum that moves through the real world, on the one hand, and an interior or underground self that is often at odds with that world, on the other. He feels under immense pressure from his contrasting but equally demanding parents, while also seeking constantly to maintain their love and favour. He shuttles between the contradictory impulses that they seem to embody: the paternal authority of his father's Protestant work ethic with its values of hard work, emotional repression, self-discipline; and his mother's more sensual and plastic interest in the aesthetic and the life of the mind. His parents are revealed as Palestinian, but long before Edward was born they were mobile and cosmopolitan, reconstructing their own histories. This sets the precedent for Edward's life to be lived in the same manner, and indeed this rootlessness becomes a structuring principle for much of Said's work also.

We see here, then, that even so cursory an examination of the beginnings of Edward Said's own life, and his autumnal reflections on those beginnings, brings out themes that will be found to recur in his critical works: the passionate identification with Conrad; the sense of a divided but also reflexive self; the dynamic oscillation between discipline and freedom, authority and resistance, rational intellect and surging will; the sense of what he would later call, quoting the great Hungarian critic Georg Lukács, 'transcendental homelessness'; the sense of the lack of a solid identity and the need to reconstruct one, over and over again.

Influences

The purpose of this chapter is, as our first extended examination of Said's writings and ideas, to sketch out the manifold influences that help shape, and also are re-inflected in, that work. Said had a long and varied career as academic critic, political analyst, and public intellectual, and he absorbed and re-processed various intellectual currents and traditions over that period. It has often been said of him, even by his admirers, that his work was characterised by eclecticism. Here, however, we may be able to discern a greater continuity than is conventionally allowed to him.

Schematically, Said's literary criticism borrowed from and was influenced by a wide variety of the critical schools and trends of the twentieth century: Romance philology, phenomenology, Western Marxism, structuralism, and poststructuralism. But he was also acutely attuned to various strands in music criticism and musicology, and he was widely read in sociology, history, anthropology, philosophy, and political theory. More than most Anglophone critics, Said practised interdisciplinarity on a grand scale. Frequently, this got him into trouble with specialists in disciplinary areas on which he cheerfully trespassed. But for Said, this kind of 'interference' was close to a kind of methodological principle. Crossing over disciplinary boundaries, bringing disparate knowledges and epistemologies into unexpected conjunction, his work is concerned repeatedly not only with the production of knowledge, but with *the conditions of possibility* of the production of knowledge. Embedded within his discussions of Orientalism, or anthropology, or literary theory, one finds a constant probing of the grounds of positive knowledge, an epistemological enquiry that is never over or fully satisfied. We will look at the intellectual movements named above one after another, and show how they appear, and are inflected, in Said's work.

Phenomenology

Phenomenology is a European philosophical tradition, usually held to have been initiated by Edmund Husserl, and numbering Martin Heidegger, Jean-Paul Sartre, Maurice Merleau-Ponty, and Hans-Georg Gadamer among its most famous adherents. Husserl, writing in the context of the First World War and socio-political unrest all over Europe, wished to establish a new basis for philosophy, one not tainted either by a fact-grubbing positivism or by a rudderless subjectivism. He argued that it was possible to 'bracket off' the 'natural attitude' of everyday common sense – a philosophical act reminiscent of that of seventeenth-century French philosopher René Descartes when he began from a position of fundamental scepticism (*Cogito ergo sum*: the only thing one knows for certain is that one is thinking) – and launch a science of consciousness. For Husserl, we may not be sure of the existence of the material world independently of ourselves, but we can advance statements about that world of objects insofar as it appears to our consciousness. Phenomenology gives priority to the description of the world of everyday lived experience in the ordinary human life-world. It is interested in these 'phenomena' insofar as they present themselves to consciousness, as 'pure' data – not in relation to their history, their specificity, their causation, or their social context.

For Husserl and phenomenology generally, the matter of *intentionality* is important. Consciousness is held always to be consciousness-of-something. To think is to think *of* something. Thought is always directed *at* something, or 'intends' something. Irrespective of the existential status of the object at issue, consciousness is 'directed'. Individuals focus on phenomena in their experience, and thereby construct them as objects. Yet we cannot assume the existence of an object simply because it has been the focus of an intention.

Literary criticism has been influenced by phenomenology by way of a number of conduits. The existentialist branch of phenomenological thought, represented most famously by Sartre and Merleau-Ponty, stresses the experience of situated, concrete, historical subjects, a theme that we shall see appear at various points in Edward Said's work. But the most notable branch of phenomenological criticism was the Geneva School, which had come to prominence in the 1940s and 1950s, and had some currency at the time that Said was working on his doctoral thesis on Conrad. Its most famous members were Georges Poulet and Jean Starobinski. This grouping – so-called because of an association with the University of Geneva – reckoned that the task of the critic was to identify and, notably when we think of Said, to *identify with*, the unique mode of consciousness suffusing a particular writer's *oeuvre*. Thus, an author's specific sense of space and time could be seen as the unifying source of his entire corpus of work, irrespective of the differences between individual works. If this seems to be a biographical criticism, we should note that the Geneva critics' phenomenological analyses work not from the life to the work, but rather from the work – the texts – back to the life, or mind, that lies behind them.

In Said's first book, *Joseph Conrad and the Fiction of Autobiography* (1966), a phenomenological approach is very apparent. Said side-stepped the New Criticism dominant in the American literary academy at the time, and showed an early interest in continental philosophy and scholarship. Accordingly, we shall find the phenomenological analytic at work in this book, but what may surprise readers who have some familiarity with Said's later and better-known work is that we shall see a theme set in place which will resonate right through his career. The Conrad book is therefore to be seen as foundational for Said: it enunciates a first confrontation with a writer who preoccupied Said throughout his life, but it also feeds into the later work in theoretical and methodological terms. Nevertheless it is also striking that Said does not here emphasise Conrad's relationship to empire in the way that his later work might lead us to expect him to do. Yet the *ways* that Said would subsequently think about such issues may be argued to be adumbrated in the early work on Conrad.

In the Preface to his book, Said notes that Conrad's collected letters 'provide us with an almost embarrassingly rich testimonial to the intensity and variety of his intellectual life'. Yet, at the time of Said's writing, these letters had been mostly ignored by Conrad scholars. Said says that he has been drawn to the letters and to looking at them as a whole, because 'it seemed to me that if Conrad wrote of himself, of the problem of self-definition, with such sustained urgency, some of what he wrote must have had meaning for his fiction'.[1] Studying the letters, Said finds that they form an organic whole, and further, that they 'fall naturally into groups that corresponded to stages in Conrad's developing sense of himself as a man and as a writer'. Probing more deeply, Said finds recorded in the letters Conrad's creation of a public persona, which served to hide and protect 'his deeper and more problematic difficulties with himself and his work'.[2] Said determines that the 'inner dynamics' of the letters seem to be paralleled in Conrad's shorter fiction. He points out that Conrad reckoned that his short stories embodied his most 'authentic' work, as he had greater control over them than over his novels. Conrad believed, Said tells us, that

> his life was like a series of short episodes (rather than a long,
> continuous, and orderly narrative) because he was himself so many
> different people, each one living a life unconnected with the others: he
> was a Pole and an Englishman, a sailor and a writer. Hence it was natural
> for him to express himself more effectively in short works[.][3]

Said hopes that he can provide what he calls an 'integral reading of Conrad's total oeuvre'. He finds that both the letters and the shorter fiction were written in what he calls a 'retrospective mode'. Accordingly, it becomes possible to read the tales 'not only as objects of literature but, with the letters, as objects that were of spiritual use and significance to Conrad the man'. The result Said hopes for is to be a 'portrait of [Conrad's] mind and work' that 'enriches and deepens our admiration for Conrad as an eminently self-aware, responsible, and serious artist'.[4]

Even in the introductory pages of the Preface, as we see above, it is very apparent to the reader that the stress here will not be on Conrad's use of literary form, or on the ideological tendencies one might read off his texts, or on the social types or political milieus he portrays in his writing. These might be the concerns of historicist or postcolonial criticism at the end of the twentieth century or start of the twenty-first century. Rather the emphasis will turn out to be on Conrad's intellectual life, on his letters and literary texts as a unified whole and as an expression of his 'mind'. Not merely this, but the texts and the letters will be seen not merely as literary objects, but as objects of 'spiritual use' to 'Conrad the man'. It is clear that this is intended very much to be a study of the modes of consciousness and of experiential life of one great writer, as they become apparent to us through his texts and letters. The writings lead us to the activity and life of the mind, in the sense that the Geneva School would have suggested.

Abdirahman Hussein, in his *Edward Said: Criticism and Society*, suggests that the Conrad book is foundational to Said's entire career and project. He illustrates this by citing two famous passages from Conrad's great novella, *Heart of Darkness*:

> Now when I was a little chap I had a passion for maps. I would look for hours at South America, or Africa, or Australia, and lose myself in all the glories of exploration. At that time there were many blank spaces on the earth, and when I saw one that looked particularly inviting on a map (but they all look that) I would put my finger on it and say, When I grow up I will go there.

> The conquest of the earth, which mostly means the taking away of it from those who have a different complexion or slightly flatter noses than ourselves, is not a pretty thing when you look into it too much. What redeems it is the idea only. An idea at the back of it; not a sentimental preference but an idea; an unselfish belief in the idea – something you can sacrifice to.[5]

For Hussein, these two passages set out the terrain on which Said triangulates Conrad. On the one hand, as illustrated in the first quotation above, there is the interest in the knowledge-producing human subject, in the rational demystification of the world, in the will-to-knowledge. Conrad intimately and firmly yokes together the practical business of exploration and the idealism and even ontology that underpins it. For the young Marlow (in *Heart of Darkness*), or even for the young Conrad (as we know that in his memoir *A Personal Record* he writes of himself in a passage almost identical to this one), to 'go there' will be an exploratory and investigative mission, but it will also be to find his proper mode of being in the world. On the other hand, the second quotation offers a stringent critique of precisely this project. Conrad is showing how this Enlightenment drive to knowledge and exploration could also produce euphemisms, justifications, and 'rationales', to cover up sordid or violent or unjust activities.

So Conrad opens for Said the crucial matter of imperialist Enlightenment and its discontents. More importantly for Said, Conrad was deeply ambivalent about imperialism. He could sympathise with its putative idealism. He could see beneath that, to its rapacity, corruption, and inhumanity. Yet he could not see, imagine, or forecast a moment when the natives would themselves become capable of making their own history, when they would win independence and achieve self-determination. Thus, Conrad's is ultimately a pessimistic and reactionary position: the relation of domination between Europeans and colonised natives is *inevitable*, and negative for both sides. As Hussein puts it, 'to Conrad, the civilized, civilizing Westerner is condemned to rule, rob, destroy'.[6]

Hussein argues that it is this unresolved tension in Conrad that drew Said's interest. Elsewhere, Said noted of T. E. Lawrence ('Lawrence of Arabia'), a figure of distinctly Conradian complexities and ambivalences, that he at one time described himself as 'a standing civil war'.[7] It is this swerving and agonised consciousness that Said sets out to explore in his first book. The modernist intricacy of Conrad's narratives, their multiple voices, their vaguenesses and ambiguities, their scepticism about almost all ideological positions, coupled as it is with a pressing need to explore those same positions, their interest in extreme situations – all of these may be read as a dramatisation of Conrad's own psychic struggles and inner conflicts. The point for us here must be, however, that even though the stress in this first book by Said is on the shifts and developments of Conrad's *mind*, this same mind is nevertheless shown involved in what would later become characteristic Saidian problematics: the book is primarily about Conrad's self-definition, as Hussein says, but it is also about the drama of the intellectual coming to that definition in contexts of psychic, physical, ideological, and cultural extremity and difficulty – imperial struggle, war, exile, cultural dislocation, and assimilation. Over and over again, throughout his career, we shall see Said grappling with versions of these problems, either elucidating the struggles of writers and intellectuals who interest him – Conrad preeminently, but also figures such as the eighteenth-century Irish writer Jonathan Swift, the great twentieth-century German Jewish exiled critics Erich Auerbach and Theodor Adorno, the Martiniquan theorist and revolutionary Frantz Fanon, the French philosopher Michel Foucault, the Trinidadian activist and writer C. L. R. James, and the French writer Albert Camus – or undergoing such struggles himself, primarily in the context of his Palestinian activism.

Joseph Conrad and the Fiction of Autobiography is a study of Conrad's shorter fiction and letters, as we have already seen, which argues that the Polish exile fashioned and refashioned a series of images of himself at a number of crucial points in his career, through a rigorous and often painful process of creative and intellectual development. This process is painful because it moves through ironies, paradoxes, and contradictions. In Hussein's words, 'Said detects in this slow fissured development of Conrad's self-realization . . . a strange marriage of irony and heroism, of egoism and self-transcendence'.[8] This veering pattern culminates in Conrad's full identification with European civilisation and humanity, and implicitly with European imperialism; but this arrival is attained at the price of the most severe self-denial and pessimism. Notably, this narrative takes place in Conrad's consciousness in the context of the most profound crisis of Europe: one only has to think of the cultural tendencies of Conrad's time – *fin-de-siècle* decadence and millenialism, modernism, high imperialism and its demise both in the Third World and in the European Great War – to realise that his attainment of a sense of being at home in mainstream European culture was achieved only in time for the whole edifice to be shattered.

Said argues that the study of Conrad's letters and fiction together reveals not so much a set of formal literary properties, but rather the psychic history of a powerful, alienated mind in the process of agonised self-scrutiny. Said identifies three phases in Conrad's career. The first of these is the longest and most important, from the late 1880s to 1912. In this time, Conrad wrote most of his greatest works – novels such as *Heart of Darkness, Nostromo, Lord Jim,* and *The Secret Agent,* along with most of his best short fiction. This period is characterised by what Hussein calls a 'groping and moral struggle'.[9] Said shows that Conrad's letters at this time display anguish and pain. The writing of this phase is marked by profound pessimism – truth is inaccessible, meaning is always layered and ambiguous, narrative conclusions are at best ambivalent. The second phase, which Said calls an 'interlude', comes with the creation of a rather comfortable public persona, that of the 'great writer', yet during the latter part of this six-year period, Conrad was overwhelmed by the horrors of the First World War. The result is fiction typified by Conrad's masterful short story 'The Secret Sharer', where the supposed hero shelters or hides a dark side or a terrible secret. This contrast of public persona and private conscience is a mirror of Conrad's own condition. For Said, Conrad's fictive resolutions at this time are as much exercises in what Hussein calls 'self-persuasion' as they are ruses to con his readers. In the third phase, from the end of the First World War in 1918 to Conrad's death in 1924, this contrast only becomes more extreme. Key terms in Conrad's vocabulary at this time include words such as 'mastery' and 'conquest'. With the end of the First World War, Conrad concludes that a major historical phase has passed and come to completion. In parallel with that resolution, there is the finishing of a major period of Conrad's own life. This sense of completion leads to a newfound feeling of serenity and maturity. Consummation has brought the ego both freedom and control. It is as if the War has allowed Conrad's psyche to purge itself of terror and anxiety. This now allows a calm and expansive view of Europe and European culture, even while Conrad recognises the devastation that the continent has experienced.

Said, therefore, shows us that Conrad combined a kind of arrogance or even self-importance with the most powerful sense that this kind of confidence only emerges through experience. Said, from the start of his career, had an inherently dialectical or paradoxical understanding of Conrad. This is what allowed him always to take the measure both of Conrad's conservatism and of his astringent critique of the modern world, his mordant sense of the barbarities of empire and his final acceptance of an imperialist worldview, his pessimistic honesty and his recognition of the necessity of the fictions or ideological frameworks by which we live.

Said's appropriation of phenomenology is at its clearest and most extensive in his first book, yet it lingers in much later work. It is there in his second book, *Beginnings*, with its interest in *intention*. There, Said undertakes a prolonged discussion of the act of initiating an intellectual project, whether that is a disciplinary transformation, or writing a novel. The emphasis on the drama of that act is derived from a phenomenological sense of the intellect. As Said puts it himself in his original Preface, beginning 'is not only a kind of action; it is also a frame of mind, a kind of work, an attitude, a consciousness'.[10] This line of argument immediately offers a bridge to *The World, the Text, and the Critic* (1983), a book which declares itself to be centrally concerned with 'criticism or critical consciousness'.[11] What we need to note here is the focus on *consciousness*. This is the trace of Said's phenomenological inheritance. What has been set out in the case of Conrad in *The Fiction of Autobiography* – the drama of consciousness – is given a more theoretical expression in *Beginnings*, and a more socio-historical expression in *The World, the Text, and the Critic*.

It is not surprising, then, to find Said opening his much later *Culture and Imperialism* (1993) by reading T. S. Eliot's famous essay 'Tradition and the Individual Talent' as a meditation on the necessity for the poet to have an historical consciousness. Eliot wrote that

> the historical sense involves a perception, not only of the pastness of the past, but of its presence; the historical sense compels a man to write not merely with his own generation in his bones, but with a feeling that the whole of the literature of Europe . . . has a simultaneous existence and composes a simultaneous order. This historical sense, which is a sense of the timeless as well as of the temporal and of the timeless and the temporal together, is what makes a writer traditional. And it is at the same time what makes a writer most acutely conscious of his place in time, of his own contemporaneity.[12]

What draws Said's attention here is not only the 'historical sense', but the fact that Eliot defines this sense as suffusing the present, as something that is indistinguishable from the present, and also as being a matter of the writer's self-consciousness. The 'historical sense' is not a sense of a process outside or beyond the writer; on the contrary, it is 'what makes a writer most acutely conscious of his place in time'. The writer's self is seen as part of a wider cultural and historical continuum. Said sees in Eliot precisely an instance of what he calls 'worldly self-situating' in *The World, the Text, and the Critic* – an elaboration of his phenomenological inheritance.

Philology

A second major influence on Said and his work has been the tradition of linguistic and literary scholarship called *philology*. The term 'philology' is derived from the Greek, and means, literally, 'love of language and learning'. It is applied to a tradition of scholarship now often seen as superseded, and reckoned to be dry and old-fashioned: the historical and comparative study of the development of languages. In the twentieth century, philology has been held to be exemplified in the lives and work of a handful of very eminent scholars: Karl Vossler, Ernst Robert Curtius, Erich Auerbach, and Leo Spitzer. But this tradition of the study of European languages and literatures goes back to the Romantic era, and then is associated with figures such as Friedrich Schlegel and Johann Gottfried Herder. In addition, the eighteenth-century Italian philosopher Giambattista Vico, who as we have already seen is a figure of crucial interest to Said, is reckoned a precursor of philology.

It is important in this context to recognise that Edward Said himself was trained not only in the discipline of English literary study, but in *comparative literature*, a disciplinary field that was long dominated by the work of Romance philologists. The origins of comparative literature are roughly coeval with those of philology: the term was first used in Charles Augustin Sainte-Beuve's *Port-Royal* (1840), though the idea is traced back to Johann Wolfgang von Goethe's *Weltliteratur* (1827).

Said's work is heavily marked by this tradition, and it is evident in *Beginnings, Orientalism, The Question of Palestine, The World, the Text, and the Critic, Culture and Imperialism*, and in one of his posthumously published works, *Humanism and Democratic Criticism*. In other words, the interest in and commitment to philology and comparative literature runs right through Said's career. But it is not merely an interest: much of the power and fertility of Said's work is derived from a tension between the traditions of philology and comparative literature, and the various avant-garde methodologies with which his name is more often associated.

Let's now look at how Said uses philology in the major introductory essay of the collection, *The World, the Text, and the Critic*. In 'Secular Criticism', Said gives a famous and moving account of the composition by Erich Auerbach of his masterpiece, *Mimesis: The Representation of Reality in Western Literature*.[13] Said, one of Auerbach's most ardent contemporary admirers, is taken by the fact of Auerbach's *exile*, at the time of his writing his great book. Auerbach was a German Jewish philologist who lost his academic position at the University of Marburg in 1935, and subsequently took up a job at the University of Istanbul, in Turkey, where he spent the war years. Auerbach went on to move to the United States, becoming Sterling Professor of Humanities at Yale University, and dying there in 1957. In the last chapter of *Mimesis*, Auerbach points out his isolation in Istanbul during the war, 'where the libraries are not well equipped for European studies'. However, he says, 'it is quite possible that the book owes its existence to just this lack of a rich and specialized library. If it had been possible for me to acquaint myself with all the work that has been done on so many subjects, I might never have reached the point of writing.'[14] For Said, the situation out of which Auerbach produced his extraordinary literary history is multiply and extraordinarily determined, and yet '[I]n writing *Mimesis*, he was . . . performing an act of cultural, even civilizational, survival of the highest importance'.

Not merely this, but to a European scholar of mediaeval and Renaissance literature, 'Istanbul represents the terrible Turk, as well as Islam, the scourge of Christendom.' Islam and the Orient were held to be both opposed to and alienated from Europe and its religious and cultural values. Accordingly,

'[To] have been an exile in Istanbul at that time of fascism in Europe was a deeply resonating and intense form of exile from Europe'.[15]

There are many themes that Said derives from this story. He is fascinated by the relationship he discerns at work in Auerbach between distance, exile, and alienation, on the one hand, and profound knowledge, on the other. The implication is that the major critical statement requires or is enabled by a distance: by the time we come to Said's major late collection of essays, this is captured simply in the linkage 'Criticism and Exile'.[16] But Said is also interested in the manner in which Auerbach – as a Jew, already marginal and vulnerable in Europe – creates a brilliant literary history of Europe as a cultural ensemble at a time when the unity and coherence of European culture seemed doomed, and from a place where that culture was inaccessible.

Furthermore, Auerbach's distance or exile is not merely literal – though that physical distance should not be underestimated for Said. It is also metaphorical. Discussing a late essay of Auerbach's, Said notes his quotation of a beautiful and haunting passage from the *Didascalicon* of Hugo of St Victor, a twelfth-century monk from Saxony:

> It is, therefore, a great source of virtue for the practiced mind to learn, bit by bit, first to change about in visible and transitory things, so that afterwards it may be able to leave them behind altogether. The man who finds his homeland sweet is still a tender beginner; he to whom every soil is as his native one is already strong; but he is perfect to whom the entire world is as a foreign land. The tender soul has fixed his love on one spot in the world; the strong man has extended his love to all places; the perfect man has extinguished his. From boyhood I have dwelt on foreign soil, and I know with what grief sometimes the mind takes leave of the narrow hearth of a peasant's hut, and I know, too, how frankly it afterwards disdains marbled firesides and panelled halls.[17]

These lines have given Said a powerful and poetic invocation of the pains and pleasures of exile, and he quotes them in several of his books. The dialectic between distance and closeness, home and exile, rootedness and alienation has provided Said with themes to which he has returned over and over again. On the one hand, criticism and interpretation are linked to distance: in the case of Auerbach, the result is *Mimesis*, regarded widely as the finest single-volume history of Western literature ever written; on the other hand, there is the wrenching pain of leaving or being denied return to the native place. The linkage of these is, for Said, unbreakable and inevitable. But Auerbach's exile was not merely geographical. As a Jewish exile in Muslim Turkey, though also a great scholar of 'the European tradition of Christian Latinity', Auerbach found himself in a cultural environment utterly different from and in many ways opposed to his own traditions. Yet the crucial move is that, out of this apparently very unpromising situation, Auerbach made a great book. In a very difficult situation, in part *because* of that situation, Auerbach made his *magnum opus*, and enacted an intellectual performance of extraordinary power and reach. In the quotation from Hugo of St Victor, Said finds expressed a certain ideal of cosmopolitanism, a comfort with the whole world as a cultural space that he often advocated as a way beyond narrow chauvinistic adherence to a national culture. Yet, when he quotes the same lines at the end of his much later book, *Culture and Imperialism*, we find Said noting also that exile is *not* a matter of utter disconnection from a home or culture; rather it is a matter of proximity to a native place of which one is fully aware but to which one may not return. Further, 'the negative freedom of real knowledge' is to be achieved by '*working through* attachments, not rejecting them'.[18] Said's interest in criticism and exile, the drama of the intellect, and cultural clash is always grounded in historical experience.

But Said's interest in and fidelity to philology and comparative literature extends further, to Vico, author of *The New Science* (1725). Said was interested in Vico's sense of isolation as an obscure Neapolitan academic, which led him to a very particular attitude to work and to intellectual activity. Vico is invoked in many of Said's books, and Said's interest in and admiration for Auerbach was in part piqued by the latter's own resort to the Italian. In the essay 'Vico: Autodidact and Humanist', published only a year after his book on Conrad, Said sets out his relationship to Vico and the Italian critic's usefulness to him and to the humanities. The essay's title captures two of the themes that are most important in Vico for Said: knowledge relating to and starting with the self; and knowledge of and derived from the human. Said locates Vico at the start of the historicist tradition of thought, with J. G. Herder and others, and then notes the waves of interest in Vico, starting off with European Romantics such as Coleridge and Michelet, and then his appropriation by the nineteenth-century historicists, from Marx and Dilthey, to twentieth-century figures such as Benedetto Croce, Ernst Cassirer, and Auerbach.

Vico always argued that the proper approach to any intellectual problem was to 'treat things at their beginning'. As Said says, Vico's beginning was himself:

> For he was preeminently an autodidact (*autodidascolo*) . . . Everything he learned, he learned for and by himself; he seems to have been convinced of his individuality and strength of mind from his earliest days, and most of the time his *Autobiography* is an account of this self-learning.

Said then argues that

> in being an autodidact, Vico was insisting with philological astuteness
> on the self teaching itself with the authority, which is its property, of its
> humanity; and this human property resides completely in an exercise of
> will... when one learns something one first performs an act of will,
> because only by willing to learn can one learn.[19]

However, this is only the first half of the process. In becoming aware of what
one learns, something further is taking place. In separating the object of the will
from the will itself, 'the mind achieves consciousness (*coscienza*)'. So, for Vico,
the end of the act of teaching is when the *principle* that underlies consciousness
is understood as such. In Said's words, what 'Vico is trying to describe is the
mind in its double aspect of active conation (or will) and passive intellect,
the mind observing and then observed by itself'. Said goes on to compare this
intellectual stance to that of the Victorian poet Gerard Manley Hopkins, but
it could equally be compared to the portrayal of Joseph Conrad we outlined
earlier.[20] It is in this sense that Said refers to the 'anchoring centre of Vico's
work' as being 'a paradigm of the disengaged, neutralized mind that is locked
in a conflict with itself.[21]

What Said takes from this discussion is the idea that perception involves
creation, and, following from this, that human perception entails creation of a
different order from that performed by God in His making of the natural world.
Vico thus suggests that the human or social world can be understood as the creation of human minds, though, as a philologist, he points out also that the concepts with which this human creativity is effected are themselves historical and
in constant evolution. This view can then be expanded into a theory of history:

> One can read history as a study in the eternal persistence of the idea of
> man's mind, and that idea, when it is temporally considered... becomes
> narrative history. Since the idea is an idea of the mind, and since the idea
> persists in different forms, then one is to view history from the
> perspective of eternal or ever-present persistence. History then becomes
> the mind considered as structure (an ideal persistent architecture) and
> as modality, or temporal modifications; above all, it is necessary to
> understand that history is neither one nor the other exclusively. It is
> neither total rest or permanence, nor is it total action.[22]

Vico conceives of God as pure mind, and suggests that as God wills, matter or
nature comes into existence. Human will does not produce nature, but does
produce an image of it. Thus human mental work is a lesser repetition of the
intention of God, but this still means that, for Vico, 'all human things (or
institutions) are created by the mind'. Yet, as Said points out, Vico has a strong

sense of the inadequacy or fallibility of these human constructions: the *New Science* can be seen as a study of the human mind, while also an enactment of the mind, and it is highly critical of itself and of human reasoning. But in this, Vico's achievement is to have 'described the mind as a thinker, and as a thought, simultaneously'.[23]

Said moves on to suggest that in the relationship between his *Autobiography* and the *New Science*, Vico 'is providing humanists with an object lesson in what it means to view verbal records'. He quotes Auerbach, 'Vico's principal and most profound literary student', as arguing in Vichian mode that 'the simple fact [is] that a man's work stems from his existence and that consequently everything we can find out about his life serves to interpret the work'.[24] Bringing his readings of the two books together, Said now condenses his argument. Vico's problem – trying to think about both objective nature and subjective human intellection – is one previously wrestled with by Descartes, Spinoza, and Leibniz: how to bring these opposites together in a meaningful relationship. But the human mind can only be certain about itself. Certainty suggests knowledge derived from observation, and observation implies will. Will 'is practically appetitive', yet Vico realises that while intellectual will has an effect on what is 'intellectual and human', it has barely any effect on nature:

> Yet the substance of thought is sense perception, which is recorded in the mind as imagery of one kind or another. Men, however, are gifted with speech, and speech, because it is associated with the mind, expresses the result of sense perception . . . Each linguistic expression represents an act of choice, of will, for in making a sound man is merely confirming a sense impression, becoming conscious of it.[25]

What Said reads in Vico here is a theory of the relationship between thought, language, reality, and history. For, as he says, history's records are primarily linguistic. Yet Vico realised that the function of language is to give meaning to man's impressions of the world, and from this it follows that in 'the very act of understanding the world man was in reality understanding himself'. Hence, the 'language that a man speaks . . . makes the man and not man the language'.[26]

Said's reading of the *Autobiography* and the *New Science* in parallel shows us that Vico himself regarded the latter book as the major work that put shape and meaning on all of his earlier life and work: 'The important fact is that Vico the autodidact teaches himself everything, and not until he has a viable universal law formulated in the *New Science* can his autodidacticism be said to have reached its objective.'[27] In a sense, Said reads the *New Science* as auto-biography, and the *Autobiography* as methodological treatise. His conclusion of this reading of Vico is that man has become an historical creature: 'He has become a historic object and in his soul, an eternal or formal one. This . . . is in the most profound sense autodidacticism.' Finally, '[M]an, Vico, has become a philological object and a philosophical one at the same time'.[28]

Vico concentrates on the human mind, and so Said notes that the 'modalities' of the mind are the matter of historical criticism, permitting us to read man's mind as an unfolding book. This is, finally, what makes Vico such a crucial model of humanistic intellectual activity for Said. Vico proposes 'an executive paradigm of the mind', with a dual potential. Firstly, Vico 'distinguishes the mind's potential for all the human sciences temporally considered as branches growing out of a central trunk whose dominating outlook is common sense or utility'. Secondly, Vico sees the potential of the mind to 'see itself everywhere in these studies; it sees them running through time, perhaps enriched, perhaps diminished at every recourse, every reappearance they make in time'.[29] The lesson of Vico is that

> The humanities . . . have their own inescapable human logic – to rephrase from Ernst Cassirer – and it is their job to perform on themselves a continued *Geistesgeschichte* that eschews both intellectual positivism, the conceit of the philologists, and universal systematizing, the conceit of the philosophers.[30]

Vico gives Said various critical tools and positions. Vico suggests, crucially for Said, that the critic's own self is his or her first resource. More subtly, Vico offers a vision of the critical self as both the subject and object of analysis. Said's reading of the *New Science* and the *Autobiography* side by side shows Vico's critical persona as understanding that it must examine itself even as it examines its objects. Similarly, Vico distinguishes between God's creation, and what he calls the world of nations, the world of human creation and intellection. It is axiomatic for Vico that humanistic criticism can and should analyse the realm of humanly created objects and institutions: the social and cultural world can be read and critiqued for its manifestations of the human mind. Furthermore, this human creation and humanistic criticism takes place in language, and in history. Accordingly, Vico, and Said with him, argues for the historical analysis of verbal artifacts. But this activity, too, must be reflexive. Just as Vico posits the mind as both thinker and thought at once, so too the Vichian critic must be prepared to see his or her own work as historical – taking place in history – just as much as the verbal records that are the object of that work.

Marxism

Said showed deep interest in the Western Marxist philosophical tradition all of his working life. Nevertheless, his relationship with the tradition is also a vexed one, and one that has given rise to some of the most vociferous controversies about his work. Said drew on the work of Marx and Engels, and then of a number of their twentieth-century philosophical inheritors, most notably the Hungarian Marxist philosopher and literary critic, Georg Lukács; the Italian Marxist revolutionary activist and political theorist Antonio Gramsci; the German philosopher and musicologist Theodor Adorno. Other writers and intellectuals that he admired and sometimes wrote about, such as C. L. R. James, Frantz Fanon, Jean-Paul Sartre, Lucien Goldmann, Raymond Williams, the Indian Subaltern historians, all were Marxists or had explicit links with Marxism, yet it was rarely this aspect of their work that Said analysed or celebrated. He was not in any thoroughgoing or doctrinal sense a Marxist critic, and he deliberately refused the label when others sought to apply it to him and his writing. In fact, he could be severely critical of Marxist critical positions and ideas. In the last years of his life, the intellectual to whose work he had the most frequent recourse was Adorno, yet it was not Adorno's Marxism – a Marxism, it must be said, of a very heterodox kind – that drew Said's attention. He maintained a tense relationship with Marxism to the end of his career.

In the essay 'Secular Criticism', a notable statement of purpose, Said positions himself vis-à-vis Marxism and Marxist criticism. He argues that to qualify the term 'criticism' with 'labels' such as Marxism or liberalism is 'an oxymoron'. To suggest that criticism should be pre-emptively allied to a school, method, theory, or political position 'is extravagantly illustrative of how the dictum "solidarity before criticism" means the end of criticism'. Not merely this, but Said argues that in contemporary America, Marxism is more an academic than a political commitment, and it 'risks becoming an academic subspeciality'. Said is dubious about the value of that commitment in the absence of organised socialism in American political society, and when leftist literary-intellectual discourse seems unable to forge effective or useful relationships with leftist political groups. Finally,

> the net effect of 'doing' Marxist criticism or writing at the present time is of course to declare political preference, but it is also to put oneself outside a great deal of things going on in the world, so to speak, and in other kinds of criticism.[31]

Rather, Said says, he has been influenced more by Marxists than by Marxism, and he goes on to suggest that Marxism, as much as any other major discourse of the twentieth century, is itself in urgent need of demystification and criticism.

Said here evinces a strong sense that what he calls 'critical consciousness' can and should be independent of great doctrinal systems and discourses, such as those of Marxism. When he says that he has been more influenced by Marx*ists* than by Marx*ism*, he means that he has been able to learn much from the work of individual Marxist thinkers and writers, without ever identifying with Marxism as a fully fledged system. He moves quickly, and some would say unjustifiably, from the concept of Marxism as a philosophical position or methodological technique to Marxism as a group or political identity – hence, his stricture on 'solidarity before criticism'. But then he moves on to make a series of important political points: American Marxism, he says, is an academic badge rather than a serious political position. It amounts to a set of academic strategies whose political import is rendered null and void by the impossibility of their articulation with the activities of a viable leftwing party in American political society. To declare oneself a Marxist is, for Said, on the one hand, to put oneself outside or beyond many important debates or ideas in the critical academy; while, on the other hand, it may be to delude oneself that one's activities in the classroom or research seminar amount to a serious or sufficient 'politics'.

Equally, for Said, rigid adherence to a putatively 'radical' theoretical position or system such as Marxism may amount to a form of inverse 'conservatism'. Specifically, he points at the tendency of many forms of criticism, not excepting avant-garde criticism, towards what he calls 'guild consciousness'. By this Said means the manner in which forms of criticism – like other discourses – become increasingly self-referential, about themselves, as they are ever-more finely elaborated; as they find institutional expression in schools, university departments, journals, conferences, books; as they accumulate adherents and advocates, as they become ever-more influential and productive; as their ideas and precepts ramify into adjoining areas of intellectual work. This narrative of the degeneration and domestication of supposedly radical theory is one to which I shall return, but it is worth saying here that it offers a very broad story that covers a great deal of Said's work, whether political or literary critical: the widening gap between, on the one hand, ideas that purport to name and refer to the 'world' but that represent, in fact, moves and counter-moves in hermetic discursive chess games, and, on the other hand, the world itself.

For now, we need to look at some of the ways in which Marxist thought functions in Said's writing. The Marxist writer he refers to most often early in his career is Georg Lukács, and he refers particularly to two books, *The Theory of the Novel*, and *History and Class Consciousness*.[32] Critical consensus tends to divide Lukács's career into a number of phases. *The Theory of the Novel* was originally published in 1916, during Lukács's earliest phase, when he had not yet made the transition to Marxism, and when he was influenced by idealist philosophers, chiefly Kant, Hegel, and Kierkegaard. *History and Class Consciousness* was published in 1923, during Lukács's first Marxist phase, and at a time when he was seeking to revitalise European Marxism by tearing away the grim mantle of dogmatic scientism and positivism that had been the philosophical legacy of Engels's interpretation of Marx, and that was the unfolding institutional undertow of Stalinist communism. In this work, massively influential upon multiple generations of Western Marxist thinkers and activists after him, Lukács sought to reconcile the dialectical idealism of Hegel – whom he termed 'the last great bourgeois thinker' – with the revolutionary materialism of Marx. In the crucial essay in the collection, 'Reification and the Consciousness of the Proletariat', he gave Said a concept that underpins much of his critical and political work.

It is noteworthy, therefore, that Said is chiefly interested in two of Lukács's early works that mark a transition in the Hungarian thinker's intellectual trajectory. In *The Theory of the Novel*, Lukács famously described the novel, in its emergence as a literary genre in the eighteenth century, as 'the epic of a world that has been abandoned by God' – a world where heroism of the kind we associate with Achilles or Siegfried is no longer possible, a world evacuated of any sense of the co-presence of the human and the divine, a world of alienation and disillusion.[33] However, in *History and Class Consciousness*, Lukács both set out an extraordinary and comprehensive description of this melancholy condition, *and* found what he considered to be a theoretical way out of it.

Lukács's formulation of the novel as the genre of alienation, disillusionment, and 'transcendental homelessness' places it squarely as the quintessential artform of modernity.[34] For Lukács, as for many other critics, the exemplary initiation of the genre is Miguel de Cervantes's *Don Quixote*. The old man at the centre of this story, under the baneful influence of romance-reading, seeks to live in the modern fallen world while adhering to the pre-modern codes of chivalry and courtly love. The novel's comedy issues from the ever-widening gap that is opened up between Don Quixote's idealism and the grimy empirical reality that he encounters on his travels. So, the novel genre is predicated on a quest that leads not to transcendence but to disillusionment, by way of the revealed disjuncture between high abstract moralism and idealism, and the gritty, often painful, corrupt, and sordid facts on the ground.

This model of demystification, associated by Lukács with the novel, is one that Said associates also with criticism itself. In *Beginnings*, he locates criticism in a situation not unlike that of the modern novelist, when it comes to making a beginning. The modern critic seeks to locate himself at a sharp angle to a tradition, not merely to insert himself into it:

> the critic faces irregularity on all sides. Because he cannot have direct recourse to tradition in solving the problems of writers like Joyce, and because his (and Joyce's) references are to other makeshift formalities of knowledge, the critic is aptly characterized in Lukacs's epithet for the

> novel as being transcendentally homeless. He begins each work as if it were a new occasion. His beginning, as much as any modern writer's beginning, takes up a subject in order to begin it, keep it going, create it. As the beginning is related to what immediately follows it, so too are the parts of his writing to one another – irregularly, assertively, eccentrically. But these relationships . . . are not consequent in any simply causal sense. Such relationships cannot be plotted, any more than the succession of voices in *The Wasteland* can be plotted; neither are they symmetrically subordinate to any fixed central point, just as *Heart of Darkness* makes a deliberate havoc of any simple scheme based on the Quest.[35]

Said here is using Lukács's insight about the novel to make a point about his idea of criticism. Just as the modernist novelist seeks to assert a break or rupture between her work and that which has come before, so Said's critic adopts an anti-dynastic position or attitude vis-à-vis the critical tradition: she seeks neither to place herself in an illustrious lineage of scholarship, nor to set up a new orthodoxy that will persist in her wake. In the manner of a Vichian autodidact, she realises that every new project she undertakes will be, and will necessitate, a new beginning. Just as Lukács sees the novel as the epic of the modern age, so Said sees criticism as a fundamentally modern and modernist activity: it is a non-linear decentred process. It is, to return to the Lukácsian metaphor, 'homeless' – not in the sense that criticism must have a literal empirical or physical home, but rather it is 'homeless' in the world of language and writing, restless, perpetually reinventing itself, perpetually starting anew, perpetually re-examining and reinstating its own conditions of possibility.

This radically modernist attitude to criticism, accordingly, bespeaks a world where there is a widening gap opening between language and its referent, between words and things, between ideality and sensuous reality. In *History and Class Consciousness*, the greatest work of his early Marxist phase, Lukács works out an extraordinary and revolutionary theory to try to overcome this rupture. The crucial conceptual hinge in this theory is the idea of *reification*. Reification is the act of conceptualising people and ideas as objects. According to Marx, under capitalist relations of production, workers are alienated from the products of their labour: the value of their work is objectified and separated from them, in the form of the commodity. Commodities circulate in the market, on the basis of relations of exchange: their value has ceased to be related to the human work that went into their making, and they seem to forge relations of exchange value between themselves. Even further, these 'market values' invade the relations between human beings themselves: between workers and consumers, the exchange relationship based on money takes the place of human interaction. People come to regard their fellows as objects or things.

For Lukács, reification is the fate of human beings and their ideas in the world of monopoly capitalism. One might say that the fetishism of commodities and the reification of consciousness are opposite sides of the same phenomenon: in the first case, the commodity is raised to the point of seeming to construct its own relations with other commodities; while, in the second case, human consciousness is reduced to the level of objectification. Capitalism, that is, manages to isolate commodity and consciousness, subject and object, from each other, so that their mutual interrelationship in the overall ensemble of human relations is hidden. However, if this interrelationship can be brought out into the open once again, then the exploitation and alienation of capitalism is revealed and can be contested. For Lukács, this exposure can be brought about by the revolutionary consciousness of the working classes. In the praxis of the proletariat, according to Lukács, there is a radical fusion of 'real consciousness' (the actual self-awareness of an individual or social group regarding its social class) and 'possible consciousness' (a class's collective awareness of its 'objective possibilities' of historical realisation), which in other classes are isolated from each other. This coalescence permits the proletariat to escape the veils of false consciousness and attain a dialectical awareness of the social totality.

So consciousness can escape the capture of reification at certain crucial moments. At a moment of crisis in the social system that is characterised by reification, the values or ideas that lie outside of the capture of the economic laws of capitalism – sentiment, passion – become themselves vital to reified thought. Suddenly the reified mind has the opportunity to see behind the apparently ineluctable portrait of society as a mere array of economic factors and inert objects. The mind can then think not merely of the lifeless reified world, but of the process by which it came to be that way. The reified mind can understand its own objectified nature, but by so doing, it can then think past it, into a possible future. The crisis has become a moment of opportunity, of dialectical analytical thought, or, as Said sees it, of *criticism*.

This moment of revolutionary consciousness is, for Said, a perfect example of radical intellectual beginnings. Discussing the beginning moment of intellectual projects, and their tendency to retroject for themselves 'an ostensible point in the past from which the present might have evolved', Said tells us that 'for the great modern rethinkers, the beginning is a way of grasping the whole project':

> As Georg Lukacs surmised in *History and Class Consciousness*, it was Marx's job to show first that the apparently immutable and object-like beginnings hitherto accepted by the forms of bourgeois thought contributed to, rather than lessened, the separation between man and

his nature. Then Marx went on to demonstrate, as Vico had demonstrated before him, man is in fact the beginning of all study, but man for whom the '*social* reality of nature, and *human* natural science, or the *natural science about man*, are identical terms'. Clearly this signals a radical displacement of traditional thought, for in order to see man as the true origin of social change a new fusion between man and his activity must be considered possible and thereby rethought in man's mind. The very act of beginning must no longer set man apart from his end, but must immediately suggest significant connections between it and man. Marx thus tied his own interpretive activity to human activity in general at a common revolutionary point of departure.[36]

Said offers us here a potent fusion of Vico, Marx, and Lukács. The stress on 'man' as the beginning of all study is the imprint of the Italian thinker's humanism. The quotation from Marx's *Poverty of Philosophy* is redolent of Lukács's theory of the fusion in the revolutionary consciousness of the proletariat of social reality and human science or knowledge. The 'displacement of traditional thought' is brought about by this combination of Vico and Lukács. The suggested linkage in Marx of interpretative activity and wider human activity is Vichian, also. Finally, interpretation is linked to revolutionary beginnings, in a manner borrowing from both Vico and Lukács.

It is important to note here that although this discussion takes place at a very high level of abstraction, these matters were practical and political, as well as philosophical, for Said. In an interview published a year after *Beginnings*, he makes this very clear: Lukács, he says, 'was attempting to show the extent to which a revolutionary gesture could be made as a sort of metamorphosis from one sort of consciousness to another'. Furthermore, Lukács suggests to Said the dangers of the reification of criticism, critics, and texts. 'To treat each of those as if detachable from the others and from society and history is to impose on them a status they have only in their weakest most rarified form.'[37]

'[B]eginnings', Said wrote later in *Orientalism*, 'have to be made for each project in such a way as to enable what follows from them.'[38] Said's interest in Lukács is that he offers a model of beginnings that is intended to make possible a radical reorientation of thought. Yet, he also used Lukács to show the fate of radical theory in the academy. Even Lukács's thought could become reified, it seems. In a 1982 essay, 'Traveling Theory', Said wrote about the ways that ideas can move from one setting to another, and how in this process they may be, and often are, transformed. Said's main concern is how putatively radical ideas can become domesticated and institutionalised. His main example is Lukács's idea of reification-and-totality. This theory was originally developed in the context of the Hungarian Soviet Republic, during its brief life in 1919, and was conceived as a contribution, at the level of theory, to that revolutionary moment. This is in marked contrast to the idea's next manifestation, in Said's narrative, in the work of the French structuralist Marxist critic, Lucien Goldmann. In his book *The Hidden God* (1955), Goldmann derives from Lukács's theory of insurrectionary consciousness an idea of 'worldview' in the work of Racine and Pascal, and in the other Port-Royal Jansenists, the relationship of their texts to the social whole. Yet as Said notes, there has been a declension in this re-working:

> The sheer existence of class, or theoretical, consciousness for Lukacs is enough to suggest to him the projected overthrow of objective forms. For Goldmann an awareness of class or group consciousness is first of all a scholarly imperative, and then – in the works of highly privileged writers – the expression of a tragically limited social situation.[39]

The next modulation of Lukács comes in the work of Raymond Williams, a Marxist or quasi-Marxist critic whom Said knew personally and admired. This admiration did not prevent him from caustically noting that no matter how interesting and subtle the use Williams made of Lukács's theory of reification-and-totality – in renewing English literary studies at Cambridge – it was nevertheless 'originally formulated in order to do more than shake up a few professors of literature'.[40] However, Said also notes Williams's ability – which he attributes to the Welsh critic's reflective distance from Lukács's revolutionary Budapest – to see the problem of how a powerful theory can become 'a methodological trap', if over-used, if used limitlessly.[41]

Said goes on to describe similar problems with the work of Michel Foucault, and its reception and adaptation by his disciples in the United States, a matter to which we turn in Chapter Three. Here it is worth noting that Said himself, after a gap of about twelve years, returned to this question, in an essay entitled 'Traveling Theory Reconsidered'.[42] In this essay, Said criticises his own earlier work for its concentration on what he calls the 'reconciling' aspects of Lukács's theory and its adaptations. If Lukács saw in 'the consciousness of the proletariat' a bringing together of subject and object, a bridging of the rift between the reified mind and its object, Said asks himself: What if the Hungarian's theory travelled into contexts and usages that *denied* that reconciliation? Would this not be an alternative, radicalised mode of 'traveling theory', one that refuses 'Lukács's desire for respite and resolution' and 'restates and reaffirms its own inherent tensions by moving to another site'?[43] Said finds his examples in the work of Theodor Adorno and Frantz Fanon.

Adorno's *Philosophy of New Music* (1948) is, for Said, 'a quite spectacular instance of a traveling theory gone tougher, harder, more recalcitrant'.[44] For the Lukács of *History and Class Consciousness*, the problem of the 'subject-object relationship' – the relationship between perceiving consciousness and that which it perceives – in modernity can be transcended by the consciousness of the proletariat, which in a moment of crisis suddenly sees the reified world for what it is. Adorno accepts Lukács's analysis of reification, but he does not project the resolution that Lukács posited in the consciousness of the workers. Adorno, writing about modern music – the early twentieth-century music of Berg and Schoenberg – argues that it is, in Said's words, 'so marginal, so rarefied, so special an expression as to represent a total rejection of society and any of its palliatives'.[45] Such music embodies the *impossibility* of the kind of synthesis to be found in the vision of the proletariat in Lukács's account. The ferocious dissonance and bristling difficulty of Schoenberg's music made it uniquely resistant to consumerism and administration. His music was art that did *not* comfort its listeners, that did not offer them a space where the alienation of the reified world could be overcome. In Said's words,

> Instead of social relevance, Schoenberg's aesthetic chooses irrelevance; instead of amiability the choice is intransigence; instead of antinomian problematics being overcome (a central notion of Lukács's history of classical philosophy) they are vindicated; instead of class consciousness there is the monad; instead of positive thinking there is 'definitive negation'.

So in the work of Schoenberg, music becomes 'what Lukács's reconciled consciousness has given up – the very sign of alienation which, says Adorno, "preserves its social truth through the isolation resulting from its antithesis to society"'.[46] The sense of regression here only becomes more striking in that Adorno, in his interpretation of Schoenberg, works remorselessly to undercut the hopefulness of Lukács's escape from reification. The composer's mastery of the atonal technique he had devised to break free of conventional music ends up dominating him:

> In Adorno's descriptions here there is a breathtakingly regressive sequence, a sort of endgame procedure by which he threads his way back along the route taken by Lukács; all the laboriously constructed solutions devised by Lukács for pulling himself out of the slough of bourgeois despair – the various satisfactory totalities given by art, philosophy, Marxism – are just as laboriously dismantled and rendered useless.[47]

What is attractive to Said here is Adorno's search for a zone of absolute resistance to reification and the alienation of consciousness under industrial capitalism. Adorno dares to posit the aesthetic as a space where resistance may be found, not in a form analogous to the heroic realist fiction so admired by Lukács, but rather in a music whose rejection of the reification both of art and of the minds of potential listeners is so thoroughgoing as to risk never being heard.

'Traveling Theory Reconsidered' is a remarkable essay in that it shows Said returning to work of the 1980s and extensively revising it. If the earlier essay, 'Traveling Theory', was pessimistic in its narrative of the decline and domestication of radical ideas, the later article is not so defeatist. Yet it is not hopeful, either. 'Traveling Theory Reconsidered' is an example of Said's work of the 1990s, written at a time when he was aware that he was suffering from what would turn out to be terminal leukaemia, and also at a time of what he considered to be a disastrous turn in the political fortunes of the Palestinians, under the terms of the Oslo Peace Process. This was a phase of Said's life and work when he was preoccupied with what he called 'late style', an idea he took from Adorno. He was at work on a book on the subject when he died in 2003, but a number of essays were published in the 1990s that would either contribute to that project or were written in a proximate mood.[48] The tendency dominating this work is one of both a greater aestheticism, but also defiance. Late style, as we shall shortly see, is not a matter for Said of reconciliation or resignation, but rather of unresolved paradox and difficulty.

However, before we come to Adorno's influence on Said, we need to look at the imprint of Antonio Gramsci. Gramsci was, roughly speaking, a contemporary of Lukács's. He was, even more than the Hungarian, an activist and union organiser. Founder of the journal *L'Ordine Nuovo* in 1919, he helped to set up the Italian Communist Party in 1921, and led it from 1924. In 1926, he was imprisoned by the Fascist government of Benito Mussolini. He died in jail in 1937.

Because of the circumstances of his life, Gramsci never produced the books he was undoubtedly capable of writing. The great bulk of Gramsci's work comes to us in the form of his *Prison Notebooks*, a massive but fragmentary series of writings on a very wide variety of topics: political, economic, philosophical, and cultural.[49] Gramsci's salient contribution to Western Marxism and to political philosophy was his analysis of the tendency of class interests in conditions of industrial capitalism to disguise themselves as cultural values, and even to become naturalised as instincts. In other words, Gramsci's work offers a particularly powerful exposure of ideology's workings in modern mass society. His term for this was *hegemony*. Living through the period of the Russian Revolution, he realised that the blockages to potential similar developments in Western Europe were not merely predicated on the coercive power of the state, but on something more subtle. If Lukács had an early pre-Marxist phase in his career, where he was influenced by thinkers such as Hegel, Kant, and Kierkegaard, so too did Gramsci, who was heavily influenced by the Italian Hegelian thinker Benedetto Croce. This idealist background helped make him sympathetic to the force of ideas in society, and allowed him to realise that the dominant classes in Western societies were able to exert a leadership and directive influence at the level of ideas as much as at the level of force. Accordingly, by hegemony Gramsci meant the ability of the ruling elite to retain power by manipulating public opinion in the realm of civil society, so as to obtain the organised consent of the masses. Hegemony has truly been achieved when the masses recognise ideas and values that actually serve the interests of the rulers of society *as their own*.

For Gramsci, hegemony was to be combated by counter-hegemony: the working-out of a new set of ideas more properly reflective of the interests of the masses. This task was the proper domain of *intellectuals*, a social category to which he gave a particular stress in his writings:

> Every social group coming into existence on the original terrain of an essential function in the world of economic production, creates together with itself, organically, one or more strata of intellectuals which give it homogeneity and an awareness of its own function not only in the economic but also in the social and political fields.[50]

Gramsci distinguishes between *traditional* and *organic* intellectuals. Traditional intellectuals are those educated persons who provide an ideological rationale for the existing status quo in a given society. Organic intellectuals are those who elaborate at the conceptual and organisational level a sense of change, of new social relations or arrangements and their legitimacy. Organic intellectuals work to give emergent socio-political movements a clear self-consciousness and a coherence at the level of ideas that will enable them to intervene persuasively in the public sphere. To this extent, intellectuals help to forge hegemony: they work to break existing hegemonies by way of critique and in debate with other intellectuals, and to make counter-hegemonies. Intellectuals, in Gramsci's formulations, are the soldiers of ideological combat.

Said deploys these ideas from Gramsci frequently in his work. He is attracted to Gramsci's sense of the materiality of culture and ideas. This underlies his first crucial deployment of Gramscian concepts, in the Introduction to *Orientalism*. There he notes the separation of civil society and political society, and the operation of culture in the former. He links cultural ideas to the creation of hegemony, a process that takes place in civil society:

In any society not totalitarian, then, certain cultural forms predominate
over others; the form of this cultural leadership is what Gramsci has
identified as *hegemony*... It is hegemony, or rather the result of cultural
hegemony at work, that gives Orientalism... [its] durability and
strength.[51]

Shortly after this passage, Said initiates a discussion of 'pure' and 'political'
knowledge that is crucial for *Orientalism* as a whole. He notes that a study of
the Russian economy is likely to be much more interesting to the governing
powers of the United States (one must remember that Said is here writing well
before the collapse of the Soviet Union) than a study of Tolstoy, yet both works
would exist in the same field – Russian studies – regardless of the individual
political attitudes of the respective writers. The point here for Said is that the
political imperative of the focus on Russia overrides the academic distinctions
between fields 'because political society in Gramsci's sense reaches into such
realms of civil society as the academy and saturates them with significance
of direct concern to it'.[52] This formulation is notable for the suggestion that
political society goes some way towards *making* the objects of its own interest:
Said preserves here the possibility – if not the likelihood – of the autonomous
production of knowledge.

Putting the point more directly, Said suggests that because Britain, France,
and the United States are or have been imperial powers, 'their political societies
impart to their civil societies a sense of urgency, a direct political infusion',
wherever and whenever matters relevant to their imperial interests arise.[53]
What this means is that, for Said, rather than the set of writings about and
attitudes to the Orient that he calls 'Orientalism' being a 'mere political subject
matter or field that is reflected passively by culture', or a simple conspiracy to
hold down the East, it is instead

> a *distribution* of geopolitical awareness into aesthetic, scholarly,
> economic, sociological, historical, and philological texts; it is an
> *elaboration* not only of a basic geographical distinction (the world is
> made up of two unequal halves, Orient and Occident) but also of a
> whole series of 'interests' which, by such means as scholarly discovery,
> philological reconstruction, psychological analysis, landscape and
> sociological description, it not only creates but also maintains; it *is*,
> rather than expresses, a certain *will* or *intention* to understand, in some
> cases to control, manipulate, even to incorporate, what is a manifestly
> different... world.[54]

In this passage, the terms *distribution, elaboration, will*, and *intention* are
stressed by Said. They between them display some of his most important

influences – Michel Foucault, Gramsci, Friedrich Nietzsche, and the phenomenological tradition. But the primary influence is that of the Italian
thinker – what Said is trying to describe here is how a text of the most arcane
aesthetic or formal qualities can function as part of a much broader ensemble
headed up and deployed in the last instance by explicitly political power.

In an essay written a few years later, 'Opponents, Audiences, Constituencies
and Community', Said deploys Gramscian ideas in the course of an argument
about the politics of literary criticism. Specifically, he suggests that in modern
Western societies the state and civil society exist in a mutually significant
articulation: civil society – the realm of culture and intellectual activity, among
other things – makes the state possible, gives it something to rule.[55] The
concomitant of this formulation is equally interesting: it means that intellectual
productions exist in a competitive field, where the prominence of any one text
or idea has been achieved at the expense of the demise of other texts or ideas.
Said concludes:

> All ideas . . . and texts aspire to the consent of their consumers, and here
> Gramsci is more percipient than most in recognizing that there is a set of
> characteristics unique to civil society in which texts . . . acquire power
> through what Gramsci describes as diffusion, dissemination into and
> hegemony over the world of 'common sense'. Thus ideas aspire to the
> condition of acceptance, which is to say that one can interpret the
> meaning of a text by virtue of what in its mode of social presence enables
> its consent by either a small or a wide group of people.[56]

This point is central to a great deal of Said's literary criticism. For Said, no
matter how 'literary', obscure, or recondite a text is, it can be seen to be
linked, even if only loosely, to the political element of its circumstances, and
can be understood as part of a hegemonic ensemble. Underpinning his wide-
ranging critical project is a confidence in the crucial stakes involved. If Said's
criticism appears relentlessly 'political', this is because he was convinced of
the public life of literary texts and of the concomitant public importance of
the practice of criticism. His Gramscian understanding of the interrelation
of civil society, intellectual activity, and political society justifies the political
burden of responsibility he places on the shoulders of the contemporary literary
critic.

Equally, Said drew upon Gramsci to show what he felt was criticism's relationship with the crucial source of authority in modern societies: the state. A
1979 essay 'Reflections on American "Left" Literary Criticism', deploys Gramsci's insights to offer a powerful critique of putatively radical American criticism. His major point is that even currents of thought such as deconstruction, in spite of their high-flown claims to a fundamental critique of Western

traditions, 'further solidify and guarantee the social structure and the culture that produced them'.[57] Ultimately, 'there is oppositional debate without real opposition'.[58] What is missing, Said tells us, is an analysis of the fundamental terrain on which criticism – indeed all intellectual activity – takes place.

Arguing in Gramsci's terms, Said suggests that every society can be analysed in terms of 'interlocking classes of rulers and ruled'. These categories are not rigid; rather society is characterised by 'a dynamic distribution of power and positions'. Drawing further on Gramsci, Said divides society into emerging and established classes, civil and political realms, subaltern and dominant powers. Yet standing over this entire ensemble is the state, the fundamental source of authority in Western modernity. For Said,

> [To] a great extent culture, cultural formations, and intellectuals exist by virtue of a very interesting network of relationships with the State's almost absolute power . . . nearly everyone producing literary or cultural studies makes no allowance for the truth that all intellectual or cultural work occurs somewhere, at some time, on some very precisely mapped-out and permissible terrain, which is ultimately contained by the State.[59]

Yet the effect of the state's authority is ambiguous: it is not merely a matter of domination. What Said takes from Gramsci is a certain 'analytical pluralism', whereby the field of culture is seen neither to be fully autonomous of the state, nor yet rigidly determined by it. Rather, the world of culture belongs

> to some large intellectual endeavour – systems and currents of thought – connected in complex ways to doing things, to accomplishing certain things, to force, to social class and economic production, to diffusing ideas, values, and world pictures.[60]

Culture, in this formulation, is a realm of ideas affiliated, however loosely, to authority conceived not as dominative, but as enabling, productive, persuasive, and effective. Further, Said picks up Gramsci's term 'elaboration' as descriptive of culture. He says it means both the 'working out' or refinement of a prior idea, and also 'the proposition that culture itself or thought or art is a highly complex and quasi-autonomous extension of political reality'. It is the dense and highly wrought richness of cultural elaboration in Western societies that makes their politics possible, and that makes for the deeply ramified strength of the state. This view, Said tells us, 'distinguishes Gramsci from nearly every other important Marxist thinker of his period':

> He loses sight neither of the great central facts of power, and how they
> flow through a whole network of agencies operating by rational consent,
> nor of the detail – diffuse, quotidian, unsystematic, thick – from which
> inevitably power draws its sustenance, on which power depends for its
> daily bread . . . Gramsci . . . grasped the idea that culture serves authority,
> and ultimately the national State, not because it represses and coerces
> but because it is affirmative, positive and persuasive.[61]

In this structure of relations, the role of intellectuals is, normally, to
win legitimacy for hegemonic ensembles of ideas and the classes they
serve.

Said's argument is that modern criticism, in spite of its formidable intellectual and analytical resources, has little to say about these facts of authority
and state power. As a counter to such a dispensation, he puts forward the task
of studying *affiliation*, 'that implicit network of peculiarly cultural associa-
tions between forms, statements, and other aesthetic elaborations on the one
hand, and, on the other, institutions, agencies, classes, and amorphous social
forces'.[62]

Affiliation is a Saidian term, but it is one that is based on Gramscian premises.
It is, he tells us, the web of relations that permits the text to maintain itself
as a text: 'status of the author, historical moment, conditions of publication,
diffusion and reception, values drawn upon, values and ideas assumed, a
framework of consensually held tacit assumptions, presumed background'.[63]
To study these relationships is to bring into visibility and relief links that both
academic specialisation and literary institutions have worked to hide: 'Every
text is an act of will, to some extent, but what has not been very much studied is
the degree to which texts are made permissible.'[64] Accordingly, to analyse a text
in terms of its affiliations is 'to give materiality back to' the ties that hold a text
in its aesthetic, social, and historical location, and that enabled its production.
This is a literary-critical project that Said advocates, that he practised in his
major texts, such as *Orientalism*, and that he reckoned went a long way towards
resisting the authority of the state.

What interests Said about Gramsci, then, is the manner in which his formulations permit an understanding of culture that is highly political – culture
is a sphere of intellectual activity that is actively related to hegemony and
authority – and yet not crudely reductive – culture is, as he says, 'a separately
capitalized endeavour', an 'historical force possessing its own configurations'.[65]
In addition, and crucially for Said, Gramsci's thought, with its stress on human
agency, places a particular responsibility on the social category of intellectuals,
in a manner quite alien to any 'vulgar Marxist' ascription of a writer's political
position to her class location.

Yet the Marxist thinker most apparent in Said's thought in the last decade of his life, Theodor Wiesengrund Adorno, is best known for the utmost priority he placed in his work on aesthetics as such. Adorno is probably the most famous, and certainly now the most highly regarded, thinker of the Frankfurt School, a group of Marxist philosophers and social theorists clustered around the *Institut für Sozialforschung*: others included Max Horkheimer, Herbert Marcuse, and Leo Loewenthal. The *Institut* was set up in Frankfurt in the 1930s, but, because of its leftwing sympathies, and also because many of its leading figures, including Adorno, were Jewish, it was forced to decamp to the United States, where it was reconstituted first at Columbia University in New York, and subsequently in Los Angeles.

Adorno's work proceeds in crucial ways from that of Georg Lukács on capitalist reification. However, there are also important differences. Lukács's principal area of cultural interest was literature, and particularly the novel; that of Adorno was the European tradition of classical music. Adorno, younger than Lukács by approximately two decades, never was a revolutionary activist as the Hungarian was, and never was sympathetic to Soviet communism. Adorno, having fled the Nazi regime to the United States, found himself gloomy about all the major socio-political regimes and systems of his time: not only tyrannical Fascism and Stalinism, but also, though in different ways, Western liberal capitalism. Lukács believed that the 'consciousness of the proletariat' permitted a revolutionary understanding, and thereby potential overturning, of capitalist reification. Adorno absorbed the power of Lukács's analysis of reification, without taking on his fundamental optimism. For Adorno, the reach of reification was so total as to render most contemporary culture merely a display of reactionary commodification. The locus of resistance that Adorno did see was the area of the avant-garde music of the Second Viennese School – Schoenberg and Berg – and certain works of literary modernism, such as the plays of Samuel Beckett.

It was with his Wellek Library Lectures on music, delivered at the University of California at Irvine in 1989, and published as *Musical Elaborations* in 1991, that Said's explicit engagement with Adorno began.[66] Even there, though, he marks out a certain critical distance from the German thinker. He notes that Adorno may no longer be a figure much attended to by contemporary musicology, and then goes on to say that 'it must fall to rank outsiders with no professional musicological reputation at stake to venture the risky, often impressionistic theorizing and descriptions' that he is offering.[67] Said compares his and Adorno's education and background, and reckons that his non-Western background does not permit him 'to assume many of the values and teleologies he takes for granted'. Yet like Adorno, Said does acknowledge 'the existence of a relatively distinct entity called "Western classical music"', though he anticipates demonstrating that it is not monolithic, and also 'that when it is talked about as if it meant only one thing it is being constructed with non-Western, non-classical musics and cultures very much in mind'.[68]

Further, Said believes himself to be extending or changing Adorno's ideas to suit his own, and re-inflecting them with a mode of thought influenced by Gramsci. Pointing to Adorno's Hegelian inheritance, which he associates with 'an inescapable historical teleology that incorporates everything in its relentless forward path', Said argues instead for 'an alternative based on a *geographical* or spatial idea that is truer to the diversity and spread of human activity'.[69]

For Said, musical practice – even the sphere of classical music – takes place in various social spaces, for various purposes and played to various audiences, and at various times. To push this complexity into 'one dialectical temporal model' is 'insufficient'. This is because music contributes to the *elaboration* of social space: we should note the return of this Gramscian term. The concert hall shares certain attributes of other cultural arenas, but it retains its own specificity, most especially because of the performative aspect of music: a book may be re-read, but a performance of a Beethoven sonata can not be 're-visited' or 're-heard'. Said's point is that the concert performance endows social space with a particular quality, because it is 'more urgent, more stressed and inflected' than literary or painterly performance.[70]

It is performance that is the focus of Said's first lecture in the series, 'Performance as an Extreme Occasion'. He accepts and works with Adorno's narrative of the ever-greater aestheticisation and social isolation of music after the death of Beethoven in 1827. For Adorno, it was his own contemporary, Arnold Schoenberg, who both absorbed the meaning of music's pattern over the century since Beethoven's death, and who in his music and in his theory deepened the separation between music and society. By an aggressively technical model of composition, Schoenberg radically evacuated music of its social content. Yet modern music, 'by its very rigor and distance from the everyday world of listeners and perhaps even of performers, . . . casts a devastatingly critical light upon the degraded and therefore meaningless world'.[71]

Having put in place a formidable image of the restraints and rigidities of the contemporary performance occasion, by way of Adorno's scathing writings about the great conductor Toscanini, Said pitches against this the career of the great Canadian pianist Glenn Gould, as an example of a self-conscious musician who worked to redefine performance. Adorno believed that Toscanini's performances dramatised the triumph of technical virtuosity over music itself, and accordingly, in Said's words, were complicit 'in the creation of a basically illiterate mass-market appetite more interested in stereotypes about "the world's greatest conductor conducting the world's greatest music" than in refined and illuminating performances'.[72] Said nevertheless believes that Toscanini's styles have dominated classical music performance:

> Out of touch with a reflective composing tradition that was never
> really his, having lost contact with the vagaries and permissiveness of
> amateurish musical practice, specialized into the ascetic discipline
> of a concert repertory based entirely on masterpieces from the past,
> Toscanini's conducting, I believe, rarified and concentrated the whole
> business several steps further, and made it for a time *the* dominant
> musical paradigm.[73]

For Said, Gould both worked within and shattered the Toscanini paradigm. What interests Said are Gould's eccentricities. In a world where 'the concert occasion has superseded the contemporary composer', this 'social configuration... has provided a wholly separate alternative for the production of music'. It is in this space that Said locates Gould. What is striking is the Canadian's ability to fill out this terrain in many directions: he retired from concert performance in 1964; he chose a repertoire at odds with the traditional work of the concert pianist; he wrote very extensively about and around his recorded work:

> The paradox is that his writings are nevertheless essential as the verbal
> counterpoint he provided for himself as a performer. Thus quite
> deliberately Gould extended the limited theatrical space provided by
> performance as an extreme occasion to one whose scope includes
> speech, time as duration, an interlude from daily life that is not
> controlled by mere consecutiveness.[74]

In the end, Said believes, Gould and his self-conscious moulding of his own career provide 'a largely but not completely new concept of what performance is all about', which functions neither as a wholesale rejection, nor yet as a total transformation of musical practice. Gould's work embodied both an extension of the reified musical sphere so potently yet pessimistically analysed by Adorno, and a powerful demonstration of rethinking and radicalism within it.

The subsequent lectures in *Musical Elaborations* follow a similar pattern: over against the powerful but despairing formulations of Adorno on music and society, Said is always to be found arguing the possibility of alternatives, variations, elaborations. As the 1990s progressed, and after his diagnosis with chronic leukaemia, Said's work became more and more preoccupied with Adorno, and with ideas taken from him. Yet the use Said made of Adorno was also evolving. For the last decade of his life, roughly, Said wrote extensively on the theme of 'late style'. This concept was one he drew from Adorno's essay, 'Late Style in Beethoven', originally published in 1937.[75] A collection of essays on literature and music working on this theme, *On Late Style*, appeared posthumously in 2006.[76] But the theme also appears in work not collected in that book (though occasionally overlapping with it). We have already seen it at work in 'Traveling Theory Reconsidered' (originally published in 1994). It is also to be found in 'On Lost Causes' (originally published in 1997), and 'Adorno as Lateness Itself' (originally published in 1995), as well as in the short book *Freud and the Non-European*.[77]

Such a treatment seems apposite in a writer who had much earlier in his career produced a lengthy treatment of 'beginnings'. But the interest in 'late style' initially seems paradoxical. One might think it strange that a critic famous for his views on the political affiliations of culture, and in particular its links with historical imperialism, should spend the last years of his career more concerned with aesthetic style and form. Yet Adorno's thought actually allowed Said a re-inflected sense of cultural politics, one attuned both to his own encroaching illness and suffering, and to the worsening situation in Palestine.

'Adorno as Lateness Itself' offers a useful capsule of this thinking. Noting that a disparate range of writers have produced striking work at the end of their careers, Said points out that much of such work tends towards redemption, recapitulation, reconciliation, or transcendence: he mentions Shakespeare, Yeats, Eliot, Proust. He is interested in the representation of age in youth we find in Thomas Hardy's *Jude the Obscure*: Jude's son, Little Father Time, 'seems like an allegory of modernism with its sense of accelerated decline and its compensating gestures of recapitulation and inclusiveness'. Said takes the eventual suicide of the boy and his siblings as Hardy's suggestion that such precocious senescence cannot survive. But in Adorno's essay on late style, he finds the bones of an argument that there can be 'ending and surviving together'.[78] For Adorno, Said says, Beethoven's late-style works dramatise a very particular juncture in cultural history: 'a moment when the artist who is fully in command of his medium nevertheless abandons communication with the bourgeois order of which he is a part and achieves a contradictory, alienated relationship with it'.[79]

Adorno is captivated by the episodic character of Beethoven's late work, 'its apparent carelessness about its own continuity'.[80] As Adorno himself put it, Beethoven's 'late work still remains process, but not as development; rather as a catching fire between the extremes, which no longer allow for any secure middle ground or harmony of spontaneity'.[81] Said tells us that Adorno's thesis is based on the premise that, at the end of his life, Beethoven realised that he was not going to achieve a wholeness or synthesis in his work, and that this 'failure' was actually the composer's 'success'. For Said, Adorno puts his finger on 'the way that Beethoven seems to inhabit the late works as a lamenting, or somehow feeling personality, and then seems to leave the work or phases in it incomplete, suddenly, abruptly left behind'. Beethoven's last works are paradoxical, in that one cannot say what holds them together, without naming the figure they add up to; yet one cannot minimise their differences, either, as to do so would be to reduce their 'catastrophic' force:

> Beethoven's late works remain un-co-opted: they do not fit any scheme, and they cannot be reconciled or resolved, since their irresolution and unsynthesized fragmentariness are not constitutive, nor ornamental or symbolic of something else. Beethoven's late compositions are about, are in fact 'lost totality', and therefore catastrophic.[82]

For Said, Adorno's concept of lateness shows him to have been 'late' within the Marxist tradition, but also to have dissolved Marxism's 'agitational force' almost entirely. Any sense of dialectical advance or progression has been drained away: Adorno's lateness is for itself, and does not herald some kind of new or alternate stage:

> Lateness is being at the end, fully conscious, full of memory, and also very (even preternaturally) aware of the present. Adorno as lateness itself, not as a Swiftian Struldbrugg, but as a scandalous, even catastrophic, commentator on the present.[83]

This formulation echoes Said's commentary, in his 1994 Reith Lectures on intellectuals, on Adorno's *Minima Moralia*. This book, composed by Adorno during his American exile from Nazi-dominated Europe, is a set of 153 fragments, published in 1953 and subtitled 'Reflections from Damaged Life'. The book's form – 'episodic and mystifyingly eccentric' – represents, Said argues, 'the intellectual's consciousness as unable to be at rest anywhere, constantly on guard against the blandishments of success, which . . . means trying consciously *not* to be understood easily or immediately'.[84] Said is drawn to Adorno not merely as an analyst of lateness, but 'as lateness itself', as a subjective dramatisation of lateness. So he reads Adorno as pitching subjectivity against totality: the style of *Minima Moralia* embodies Adorno's subjectivist rejection of false totalities, false universalist understandings of social phenomena. Adorno, for Said, is an analyst of modernity who exemplifies that condition in his very style. Not for the German thinker the reconciliation of subject and object projected by Lukács: Said argues that Adorno explicitly unravels the history of efforts to effect that reconciliation set out by Lukács.[85] Modernity is a condition of unresolved contradiction and alienation, and Adorno has no faith that the 'consciousness of the proletariat' can overcome it. To produce such reconciliation is itself a falsity that could only happen under duress.

Said argues that Adorno was both of his time and apart from it. His work is 'like a contrapuntal voice intertwined with fascism, bourgeois mass society, and communism, inexplicable without them, always critical and ironic about them'.[86] Adorno may have written scornfully of reflex political 'activism', but to him, 'the uncompromisingly critical thinker, who neither superscribes his conscience nor permits himself to be terrorized into action, is in truth the one who does not give in'. Critical thought itself has a resistant, persistent, irreducible core:

> Whatever was once thought, however, can be suppressed, forgotten, can
> vanish. But it cannot be denied that something of it survives. For
> thinking has the element of the universal. What once was thought
> cogently must be thought elsewhere, by others: this confidence
> accompanies even the most solitary and powerless thought.[87]

In the end, Said's Adorno is a 'late figure' because his work so often 'militates ferociously against his own time'. Adorno criticised the major advances in every intellectual field to which he contributed. He even 'opposed the very notion of productivity by being himself the author of an over-abundance of material', which yet could not be reduced to an Adornian method or system. Lastly, Adorno's untimeliness issued in his absolute refusal ever to render his thought easily assimilable, in terms of mood, or intellectual position, or political programme.[88]

Theodor Adorno functions in Said's work as an exemplar of ultimate intellectual intransigence. As Said moved further into illness, and as the situation in Palestine got ever grimmer through the 1990s, right through the vaunted Oslo 'peace process', one suspects that he found himself taking some comfort in aesthetic experience – in music, in particular. It is worth noting that Said published more about music during this period than at any earlier phase of his life. Reading Adorno and theorising late style, writing his memoir of his early life in Palestine, Lebanon, and Egypt, and developing musical projects with Daniel Barenboim, Said identifies powerfully with the German philosopher.[89] Interviewed in 2000 by the Israeli newspaper, *Ha'aretz*, Said startlingly remarked: 'I'm the last Jewish intellectual . . . The only true follower of Adorno'.[90] A resolutely anti-dynastic thinker, Said was not given to hero-worship. His claim here is neither a joke nor hubris. The point of the remark is its function as a figure of Said's sense of his own paradoxicality, his own untimeliness, and his stubborn and rigorous isolation from the chorus of approval of the Oslo process in the West, from the corruption and autocracy of the Arafat-led Palestinian Authority, and from the slow, incremental but unrelenting violence of Israeli control and settlement of the Territories; his sense of the need to preserve a space, no matter how lonely, for criticism and negation. At a time when Said himself felt ever-more embattled and out of synchrony with his various contexts – intellectual, political, aesthetic – Adorno gave him a set of possibilities and a confidence in his own ability to dramatise the antinomies of his situation.

Poststructuralism

Structuralism is a mode of thought that became important on the French intellectual scene in the early 1960s. Perhaps the most notable aspects of structuralism as a trend were its origin in linguistics in the early twentieth-century work of the Swiss writer Ferdinand de Saussure and its ability to move into and influence other disciplines and fields. So we find that structuralism's leading figures have spanned these disciplinary areas: Claude Levi-Strauss (anthropology), Jacques Lacan (psychoanalysis), literary criticism (Roland Barthes), Marxist philosophy (Louis Althusser), and the history of ideas and disciplinary practices (Michel Foucault). Saussure's most famous and important argument was *the arbitrary character of the linguistic sign*. By this he meant that, for example, there is no necessary connection between any word, and the object or idea we customarily refer to by that term. Philosophically, the result of this thinking was to suggest that the relationship between language and meaning is a matter of convention, and that therefore language can be looked upon as a self-regulating meaning-production mechanism, one that is completely independent from human intentions. Furthermore, for structuralism, language should be analysed *synchronically*, rather than *diachronically*: as a complete system at any given moment, rather than as one that evolves over time. This permitted figures such as Barthes and Levi-Strauss to view other media of communication as if they were 'languages'. So Barthes became famous for his studies not only of literature, but also of the mass media, advertising, and the fashion industry. Levi-Strauss offered interpretations of a wide variety of practices by 'primitive' peoples, by understanding those practices as codes structured in the manner of a language.

By the late 1960s, however, thinkers such as Jacques Derrida, Gilles Deleuze, and Michel Foucault were starting to move away from and critique this line of thought. Derrida argued that meaning in language is much more unstable than structuralist thought had hitherto suggested, and the deconstructive mode of critique with which his name is associated consists in activating the hidden meanings inherent in given terms or concepts. Deleuze and Foucault, with differing inflections, argued that language and meaning are historical, are suffused with elements of power, and could not be understood merely as calmly self-organising systems.

Edward Said was one of a number of major figures in American criticism – others would include Paul de Man, Fredric Jameson, and J. Hillis Miller – who led the Anglophone response to this fertile current of French thought in the late 1960s and early 1970s. Though he wrote about Derrida, Lévi-Strauss, and, to a lesser extent, Lacan, Althusser, and Deleuze, I shall deal here only with Said's relationship with the thinker in the structuralist and poststructuralist tradition to whom he is most frequently linked – the philosopher and historian of ideas Michel Foucault. Said's work, especially *Orientalism* (1978), has often been seen as crucially influenced by Foucault, and indeed *Orientalism*'s success and impact on thought in numerous disciplines rivals that of Foucault's own works. Along with figures such as Paul Bové and Hayden White, Said was one of the major mediators of Foucault's thought into the American academy in the 1970s. Yet careful examination of his first engagements with the French thinker reveals that Said was always heterodox in his absorption of Foucault's ideas, and he was already providing a powerful critique of Foucault even before the latter's influence in the humanities and social sciences had reached its height in the 1980s.

Foucault, who was born in 1926, rose to prominence in the 1960s on the strength of a series of innovative studies of various social institutions and academic disciplines. In *History of Madness* and *The Birth of the Clinic: An Archaeology of Medical Perception*, he argued that the practices and linguistic strategies used in the incarceration and study of the insane and the sick since the late seventeenth century functioned as much to produce their objects as to discover them. In *The Order of Things*, Foucault produced a bold history of three major disciplines in the human sciences: biology, linguistics, and economics. Underlying the production of knowledge since the Renaissance have been, according to Foucault, a series of *epistemes*, or structuring codes. The shifts from one code to the next have not been linear and progressive, as the conventional post-Enlightenment 'history of ideas' would have us believe. Rather, for Foucault, the changes have been abrupt, and total. He argues that the overall system of discourse in a given historical period is an organised assembly of relationships which stands beyond the individual statements or texts which are part of it.

So for Foucault, the formation of knowledge at any given time is both enabled and constrained by an underlying master-code. The work of individual scientists and scholars is shaped by this code or structure, rather than its being shaped by them. One of the most radical implications of Foucault's work, therefore, is the suggestion that man's accumulating knowledge of himself does not result in affirmation of the self-analysing rational and transcendentally free subject beloved of traditional post-Renaissance European humanism. The figure of 'Man' is not the creator of economic, linguistic, or biological knowledge; rather it is created by those discourses. Emulating Nietzsche, who famously announced the death of God at the end of the nineteenth century, Foucault forecasts the 'death of Man'.

In the 1970s, Foucault's work turned more explicitly to social and political institutions and practices, as against academic discourses. In *Discipline and Punish*, he traced the conceptual underpinnings of the various ideas and practices of what is now called criminology. In *The History of Sexuality*, he examined the 'confessional' rationale behind the rise of sexology and its definitions – both psychiatric and juridical – of 'perversion'. Overall, then, one can say that his work manifested two particular sets of interests: firstly, he was interested at the level of methodology in the structures of possibility of knowledge; secondly, he was interested in how these structures underpin the institutionalisation of humanistic knowledge in the interests of domination and carceral control. Humanistic knowledge disciplines are revealed to be radically concerned with the *disciplining* of human subjects, in often apparently *inhuman* ways.

Said's interest in Foucault has been principally in the relationship between knowledge and power, and this theme is worked out at length in *Orientalism*, Said's most influential book. Yet it is important to realise that Said's interest in Foucault was already an important part of *Beginnings*, and it is that early interest we shall examine here. In that book's penultimate chapter, '*Abecedarium Culturae*: Absence, Writing, Statement, Discourse, Archaeology, Structuralism', Said gives an enthusiastic – but not uncritical – exposition of the methodological potential of Foucault's archaeological project. He is less interested in the specifics of Foucault's studies of madness, medicine, and the human sciences, than in the research methodology he reckons those works embody and offer. Said sees the work of the structuralists, and of Foucault in particular, as responding to the mid to late twentieth-century breakdown in the organising concepts of knowledge. For structuralist thought, Said tells us, 'knowledge is conceived of . . . as radical discontinuity', as constituted by difference. The method of producing knowledge is 'postnarrative', a 'form in which discontinuity, dispersion and rarefaction' are essential elements: 'The contemporary need for a beginning . . . testifies to an active search . . . for a non-narrative way of dealing with nonnarratable units of knowledge.'[91] The act of apprehending knowledge is *constitutive* of its objects. Nevertheless, underlying these principles of discontinuity is the supposition that rational knowledge is possible.

Said notes Foucault's affinity with Nietzsche, though, characteristically, it is the philological Nietzsche that Said stresses. He compares Nietzsche's sugges-tion that the historical sense is a disease of history to Foucault's 'constitutive ambivalence toward history'. Both Foucault and Nietzsche see man as disin-tegrated by the historical sense, and both are radically anti-dynastic thinkers, whose relationship to their discipline is 'not the continuation of a line from privileged origin to present consciousness'.[92] Rather, Foucault's thought is most concerned with relationships of *adjacency, complementarity,* and *correlation.* Said notes that Foucault is not at all gloomy in his figuration of the dissolu-tion of the concept of man; in fact he is brisk, thorough, practical. However, there is also a paradox at the heart of Foucault's demeanour in his work: 'The impersonal modesty of Foucault's writing coexists . . . with an unmistakable tone of voice that can deliver both insight and learning.'[93] This contradiction – between the force and imprint of Foucault's personal style, and the anti-humanism of the project he articulates through that style – is a hint of what will become the focus for Said's later critique of Foucault. But in *Beginnings,* Said is content to show us that Foucault 'makes one aware that writing, books, and authors are concepts that do not always entail one another in exactly the same way'.[94] Foucault disperses the conventional categories of criticism. What is particularly compelling to Said is that this shattering is effected by historical means.

Yet Foucault's 'history' is unorthodox, also: 'Foucault cares more for histories than he does for History.'[95] Said notes that Foucault's programme of 'archae-ological' research is moved by three major imperatives: chance, discontinuity, and materiality. As Said puts it himself, 'Foucault intends the reinclusion into thought of elements that had been banished as disruptive ever since Plato. He argues furthermore that Hegel's dialectic so compelled thought into continu-ities that any radical philosopher since Hegel has to think against Hegel.'[96] The point here is that Foucault's archaeology assaults or overturns traditional histo-riography: the stress on chance undermines models of historical causality; the stress on discontinuity breaks down notions of linear and progressive historical narrative; and the stress on materiality permits a focus on the functionality, force, and effects less of ideas themselves than of language as discourse:

> Thus the roles of the founding subject (*le sujet fondateur*), of originating
> experience (*l'experience originateur*), and of universal mediation
> (*l'universelle mediation*) have been to embrace and legitimate a
> philosophical ideology in which discourse is a servile instrument of
> thought and/or truth, but never an ongoing reality with a behavior
> (*discursivity*) of its own.[97]

Foucault's attitude is the reverse of this. His work argues for a move away from the idea of the founding subject, for the inaccessibility of originating experience, and for a focus on specificities rather than on universals. Not merely this, but Foucault is recognised by Said as inverting the relationship between knowledge and truth: where truth was formerly reckoned to be the goal of knowledge, now it is seen to be a mere function of knowledge. The critique of the subject in Foucault also has the most profound ramifications:

> Not only has the subject guaranteed ideas of priority and originality, but also ideas, methods, and schemes of continuity and achievement, endowing them libidinally with a primal urgency underlying all patterns of succession, history, and progress. History in the main has acquired its intelligibility through a kind of anthropomorphism projected onto and into events and collectivities of various sorts; these are then thought of as functions of a subject, and not vice versa.[98]

Said suggests that Foucault is the 'founder of a new field of research (or of a new way of conceiving and doing research)'. Foucault's work of 're-presentation and reperception of documentary and historical evidence' is so distinctive as to have made for itself 'a new mental domain' – neither history nor philosophy – and 'a new habit of thought'. Foucault has devised 'a set of rules for knowledge to dominate truth, to make truth as an issue secondary to the successful ordering and wielding of huge masses of actual present knowledge'.[99]

Said here echoes Foucault's own designation of certain master thinkers, such as Freud and Marx, as 'founders of discursivity' – the instigators of an entire line of thought.[100] Yet this estimation of Foucault and his impressive 'new mental domain' and 'new habit of thought' does not prevent Said from recognising that these entail the demotion of a Platonic ideal of truth, and the elision of the subject: as Said quotes Foucault, '[I]t involves risking the destruction of the subject of knowledge in the infinitely deployed will to knowledge'.[101]

Following Foucault's 1970 inaugural lecture at the Collège de France, Said sets out what he sees as four principal methodological tenets of Foucault's work: (1) *reversibility*; (2) *discontinuity*; (3) *specificity*; and (4) *exteriority*.[102] By *reversibility*, Foucault means that rather than seeing such concepts as authorship or a discipline as foundational – as the origin of discourse – the critic should view them as *functions* of discourse, as moments where discourse exerts its own power of regulation and control. When an author seeks to insert herself into a particular field, she must do so in accordance with certain rules of writing, subject matter, organisation, terminology, and analytical approach.

By *discontinuity*, Foucault means that there is no final unitary level of truth to be discerned through the veil of discourse by the penetrating intelligence of the critic. Rather, all that is there to be found is another or more or different discourses. In Foucault's work, as Said points out, this applies particularly to history. Foucault, Said tells us, 'cares more for histories than for History'; instead, in Foucault's view, 'history is but one discourse among many'. Said's reference to 'History' is to the progressive unitary humanistic conception of history derived from the Enlightenment, and from Hegel in particular. But the Foucauldian idea of history as discourse has serious and interesting implications. When language takes on the kind of materiality that Foucault seeks to give it, then 'the past... becomes only the cumulative repetition of designated words'. Further,

> Such a past lasts only so long as its elements – which make the past possible, and not the other way around – are of value. Thus each epoch defines its forms and its limits of expression, of conservation, of memory, of the reactivation of preceding cultures or foreign ones, of appropriation. And since the very notion of an epoch is itself a function of these limits and forms, it is even more accurate to say that each discursive formulation articulates the limits and forms of its own existence, inseparable from others.[103]

Thus, Said would argue, Foucault's histories are characterised by multiplicities, but also by a sense that every epoch's sense of itself is linguistically determined and thus, one might say, introverted. If the past has become a linguistic or textual object, then the study of the past, and the reasons for studying that past, have been seriously undermined. Foucault seems to write histories, but in fact there is a real sense that he writes philosophical treatises of which the stage props are historical moments and evidence.

By *specificity*, Foucault means that discourse must be analysed for what it is in itself, not for any sense of another realm of reality or phenomena which it is secondary to or represents. It must not be assumed that the world is so shaped as to deliver itself up to discourse; rather, in fact, discourse must be understood as a kind of violent or appropriative act. The most obvious way that this idea works is in its resistance to the tendency in literary studies to move immediately away from a statement – a speech, a book – towards an *author*, to understand the origin and meaning of a text as proceeding chiefly from the human subject. Foucault is much more interested in the sense that such a statement finds its significance in its location vis-à-vis a wider but anonymous body of similar statements. Externally, a discourse can be defined by its exclusions: those things it rejects or wishes to extrude: the wrong, the untrue, the irrational. Internally, a discourse has rules and guidelines that permit it to constitute, define, order, and produce a taxonomy of its objects.[104]

A discourse must also have rules that allow for its *transformation* – discourses emerge out of specific and determinate conditions, and move into a future that will be characterised by other, new conditions. Further, there must be principles of *correlation* – discourses exist in enabling relations with other discourses and institutions. Clinical medical statements compose a clinical medical discourse, but that also lies in proximity to discourses of biological science, psychology, and philosophy; furthermore, it exists in relation to nondiscursive arrangements and structures, such as political, economic, and social formations.

Lastly, for Foucault, *exteriority* means that the critic must not seek to penetrate to the 'heart' of a discourse, but rather look to the conditions of possibility that lie outside the discourse. Foucault is interested in examining the forms of discourses or disciplines, at least as much as he is concerned with their content. More to the point, he is convinced that the form of a discourse is a crucial part of its content – its linguistic surfaces are vital indicators of its overall significance.

Crucial to Foucault's radically revisionist mode of approaching history and evidence is his focus on ideas or thoughts as *events*. He seeks to understand them 'precisely, consciously, painstakingly as being mastered in his writing in their aleatory and necessary character as occurrences'.[105] Said is interested in the manner in which Foucault's method results in thought being conceived as taking place not only at a temporal moment, but in an epistemological *space*. To 'think' a discursive event, Foucault needs to advance simultaneously on several fronts. He needs to describe the field, or episteme, where this event occurs. At the same time, he needs to explain the nature of the 'statement-event', what relationships subsist between such events, and the kinds of results or changes such events can effect. Lastly, he has to set out a way of accomplishing such tasks.[106] Thus,

> Foucault's analysis aims to describe the curve of motion that goes from a statement occurring as a singular irruption to a statement as variation in discourse. The same curve would describe the relationships between one discourse and others, between one episteme and other epistemes, each singularity assimilated to a larger order with more or less violence; this is how the intransigent aleatory character of an event is reduced, although never destroyed completely.[107]

Said notes Foucault's use of the image of the theatre to describe his combination of philosophy and history. The theatrical or dramatic metaphor suggests, firstly, the methodological self-consciousness of Foucault's work; and, secondly, it suggests that the effect of that work is to locate thought in a three-dimensional and spectacular space. As Said explains, 'this precisely fits Foucault's attitude toward what he calls the existence of discursive events in a culture, their status as events, and also their density as things – that is, their duration and, paradoxically, their monumentality'.[108]

Thus we can say that Said is attracted by a number of features that he identifies in Foucault's project. He is interested in the French thinker's stress on language, not simply as a medium for the representation of human ideas, but as an active and material force in the world itself. Along with this goes Foucault's constant recursive reflection on the grounds of possibility of knowledge itself. Said recognises fully the power and innovation in Foucault's capacity comprehensively to rearrange the traditional discipline of 'the history of ideas'. Language is both the first enabling condition of knowledge, and its final restriction. These are attributes that he shares with Vico, though Foucault's abandonment of the human subject as the agent of history separates them, and lies behind Said's later severe critique of Foucault. More specifically, Said finds Foucault's effort to describe ideas and texts in terms that are not simply historical deeply compelling. For Foucault, as we saw, a text is a kind of event, and an event occurs at a certain time and in a certain place; it has a certain duration; it produces certain effects. This sense of textual development, persistence, and result is crucial to Said's idea of the 'worldliness' of texts, as it is developed in books such as *The World, the Text, and the Critic* and *The Question of Palestine*, though Said gives this concept a much harder materialist edge than Foucault.

Yet even at this early stage Said shows some unease in his reaction to Foucault. This does not appear in the form of open critique – his attitude is generally one of admiration and interest. The unease, which is worth noting here as it hints at the full-blown critique to come, manifests itself obliquely. Said notes Foucault's challenge to the subject, which cuts directly across his own phenomenologically derived interest in consciousness and intentionality. He points out Foucault's radical assault on history conceived as a coherent, linear, teleological project driven by human agency. And Said reveals to his readers the implications of Foucault's image of knowledge as organised by vast trans-subjective structures such as epistemes and discourses for a Platonic conception of truth itself. Said's unease also shows in the ways that he discusses Foucault in terms that the French writer would have rejected. When Said tells us that Foucault's 'angle of vision' is 'a highly disciplined and coherent viewpoint that informs his work to such a degree as to make it *sui generis*, original', he must immediately admit that this is 'a claim Foucault himself would not make for it'.[109] Said here is, wilfully, describing Foucault in very un-Foucauldian terms. This is the same Foucault that Said has correctly described as an admirer of Beckett, and more specifically of the subject dissolved in language in Beckett.[110] The unease is displayed in

Said's persistent stress on Foucault's own personal qualities as a writer – his tone and style. It is there in Said's description of Foucault in terms derived from phenomenology, as when he suggests that Foucault is 'a consciousness completely awakened to and possessed with the troubled conditions of modern knowledge'.[111] Phenomenology is a philosophical system whose exorbitance of consciousness and the subject is the antithesis of Foucault's remorseless hollowing-out of these categories. Said's unease is made manifest in his wish to compare Foucault's work to the philological work of Nietzsche: in this gesture, he rightly pinpoints Foucault's powerful interest in the German thinker, but at the same time he strategically recuperates Foucault for the much older tradition of Romance philology.

Said's early reading of Foucault is symptomatic of his deployment of his intellectual influences generally. He never subscribes to any one school or method comprehensively. For Said, method and theory are never to be raised to the level of rigid principle. Always there is the risk of a theory or method losing touch with its often radical beginnings and becoming a sealed, self-contained mechanism and, at that point, Said moves on. Often also, as with his treatment of Foucault, there is the effort in Said to reconcile bodies of thought that appear profoundly antithetical to each other: Marxism with poststructuralism, poststructuralism with Vichian or Romance philology. What is undeniable is that, from his manifold influences, Said forged a productive body of critical work, and it is to that sense of his works we shall turn now.

Chapter 3

Works

Edward Said's working career was characterised by a number of features: (1) the variety of his interests; (2) the unorthodox academic or disciplinary pattern; (3) the willingness to step outside of his declared area of specialisation; (4) the interest in the politics of the Middle East. In literary-critical terms, he wrote across the entire span of Western literature, from Euripides to George Orwell. He only wrote one conventional monograph (usually defined as a single-author study), his book on Conrad. The Polish writer would recur in Said's writing, in numerous later books, but Said would never again devote an entire study to just one writer. Thereafter, we get a complex and rich meditation on intellectual history, as dramatised in a wide variety of European nineteenth- and twentieth-century fiction and criticism (*Beginnings*); an extraordinary critique of Western images and knowledge-production of the Arab Orient, in literature, history, travel-writing and policy-formulation (*Orientalism*); a major intervention into Western ideas about the Palestine question (*The Question of Palestine*); essays largely concerned with the conditions and possibilities for literary criticism (*The World, the Text, and the Critic*); polemical essays on Palestine (*Blaming the Victims*); a meditative book on Palestinian life, especially exile (*After the Last Sky*); a massive study of empire and culture, significantly moving on from *Orientalism* (*Culture and Imperialism*); essays on music and opera (*Musical Elaborations*); an unfolding concern with 'late style' (*On Late Style, Freud and the Non-European*); and four volumes of political essays (*The Politics of Dispossession; Peace and Its Discontents; The End of the Peace Process; From Oslo to Iraq and the Roadmap*). This is, by the standards of academic literary scholarship and criticism, a highly irregular, not to say illegitimate, pattern, but it is also, in part, what makes Said interesting. One notes that the interest in culture and politics is particularly evident from *Beginnings* (1975) onward, though it was present at essay length previously. One notes that there is a move from what one might term purely professional work (*Joseph Conrad and the Fiction of Autobiography*, *Beginnings*) out to openly political work in the texts on Palestine, but also out to non-literary material such as music. One notes also that with books like *Culture and Imperialism* (published by the non-academic presses Knopf in America and Chatto and Windus in Britain), Said was increasingly moving out to address wider, not purely academic, audiences. This reflects Said's status as a globally significant intellectual by the 1990s, but it is also a trajectory whose early form was visible though submerged in the work of the 1970s.

To offer an account of all of Said's work would clearly require a much longer book than this one, so it is inevitable that some ruthless choices have here to be made. What this chapter will do is discuss a cluster of books that are crucial to an understanding of his work, with some discussion of essays and materials from beyond that. The vital books are *Beginnings*, *Orientalism*, *The Question of Palestine*, *The World, the Text, and the Critic*, and *Culture and Imperialism*. Other works will be discussed in relation to these.

Beginnings: Intention and Method (1975)

Beginnings is Said's first major work, and, as I suggested in Chapter Two, it is not only a substantial book in itself but also sets out a number of themes and interests for Said in his later work. In the early 1990s, Timothy Brennan (one of Said's most acute commentators) suggested that Said had spent much of the period between the publication of *Joseph Conrad and the Fiction of Autobiography* and that of *Beginnings* engaged in meditation on a 'deliberately repetitive elaboration of *how* to write and speak as a public person: that is, not simply his view that being a public intellectual is a good thing, but his prolonged enquiry into the mechanics of being so'.[1] Brennan is drawing our attention to the manner in which, in several of his most important books – *Beginnings*, *Orientalism*, *The World, the Text, and the Critic*, *The Question of Palestine*, *Culture and Imperialism* – Said sets out at the onset, again and again, to discuss the conditions of possibility of the intellectual-political project in hand. Each book starts with a 'meditation on beginnings', one might say. However, the difference with *Beginnings* itself is that it stands in this relationship to much, if not quite all, of the rest of Said's career.

The publication of *Beginnings* was a major academic event, and the distinguished literary-critical journal *Diacritics* brought out a special issue almost wholly dedicated to Said's book, including a long interview with Said.[2] The interview reveals many of the subsequent constants of Said's writing: the issue of 'worldliness' (Said published 'The Text, the World, the Critic' in 1975, later renamed as the famous essay 'The World, the Text, and the Critic'); the interest in Frantz Fanon and the idea of 'Orientalism', gesturing towards the 'post-colonial' Said yet to come; the critique of the domestication of supposedly radical 'theory', including the poststructuralist theory then in the ascendant in the Anglophone academy; and the sense of being a committed, political intellectual.

It is important to note that *Beginnings* is itself a self-conscious text. It is not only a discussion of beginnings: it is also aware of the ironies and exigencies of being a 'beginning' itself. The book opens with a short chapter entitled 'Beginning Ideas', and here Said offers his first definition of a beginning: 'the beginning is the first point (in time, space or action) of an accomplishment or process that has duration and meaning. *The beginning, then, is the first step in the intentional production of meaning.*'[3] Said notes the cluster of terms that surround the idea of beginning, and that are also germane to a cultural-intellectual project of this kind: *innovation, novelty, originality, revolution, change, convention, tradition, period, authority, influence.* These terms will have resonances throughout the book. Said sets out the initial problematic as it might affect a critic, though his argument applies to any kind of writing:

> When I first became interested in beginnings several years ago, some of the problems struck me as essentially constituting the professional dilemma of the writer interested in 'literary criticism': How should he begin to write? I then discovered that this question conceals at least four others: (1) after what training does one begin to write? (2) With what subject in mind does one begin to write? (3) What is the point of departure for writing – a new direction or one continuing from old ones? (4) Is there a privileged beginning for a literary study – that is, an especially suitable or important beginning – that is wholly different from a historical, psychological, or cultural one?[4]

If a 'beginning' initiates 'the intentional production of meaning', then we need to examine the term 'intention'. By this, Said refers to 'an appetite at the beginning intellectually to do something in a characteristic language – either consciously or unconsciously, but at any rate in a language that always (or nearly always) shows signs of the beginning intention in some form and is always engaged purposefully in the production of meaning'. Said tells us that 'intention' has at least two other suggestions. Firstly, that 'intention is the link between idiosyncratic view and the communal concern'. Secondly, intention is an idea 'that includes everything that develops out of it, no matter how eccentric the development or inconsistent the result'.[5] If these formulations seem circular or self-confirming – the beginning starting the intention, the intention emerging at the beginning – then this is correct: J. Hillis Miller, responding to *Beginnings* in a review-essay in that *Diacritics* special issue, put the matter thus:

> What 'cannot be said' in *Beginnings*, without making the production of the book impossible, is just those latent aporias about the self and its intentions, about history, and about beginnings, out of which the book constantly goes on producing itself, like a mushroom out of its mycelium.[6]

Beginnings is a volume of six chapters. The first chapter, 'Beginning Ideas', introduces the broad theme of the book, yet even there, Said declares that the real 'beginning' of his book is the second chapter, 'A Meditation on Beginnings'. There follows a long chapter on the modern novel, 'The Novel as Beginning Intention', after which we get 'Beginning with a Text', 'Abecedarium Culturae: Absence, Writing, Statement, Discourse, Archaeology, Structuralism', and, finally, 'Conclusion: Vico in His Work and in This'. There are a number of ways of looking at the book. It has a quasi-historical structure: Chapter 3 deals with what Said calls 'the classical novel', by which he means the novel from the eighteenth century up to the late nineteenth century. In Chapter 4, Said 'treats beginnings as aspects of the function of what we may call the postnovelistic text', moving into and beyond novelistic modernism, but treating issues of modernism in texts not conventionally considered as literary. Chapter 5 stages Said's decisive confrontation with the (at his time of writing) most recent critical theory of texts: French structuralism and poststructuralism of the mid to late twentieth century. As we saw in Chapter Two of this book, the writer Said is chiefly interested in here is Michel Foucault, though he also discusses Jacques Derrida, Gilles Deleuze, Claude Levi-Strauss, and Louis Althusser. The final chapter of *Beginnings* is an adapted and expanded version of 'Vico: Autodidact and Humanist', which shows how Vico has been crucial to Said's overall approach.

But the historical narrative implied here is only part of the book, and indeed to describe it in narrative terms is to do violence to the book's purpose. For Said's book is a *performance* as much as an account or an analysis. It embodies many of the ideas it wishes to put across. Said announces that 'the inaugural meditative essay sets forth an intellectual and analytical structure for beginnings, a structure that moreover enables and *intends* a particular philosophical and methodological attitude towards writing'. The subsequent chapters deal with beginnings in fiction and criticism, where it is stressed that 'there is an equal emphasis upon *what* the work in question begins and *how* that beginning implies, on the critic's part, a particular methodology for understanding that kind of work'.[7] But if the book is patterned as a series of investigative meditations, this means that it is mistaken to look to it for a conventional interpretative narrative, or for a conventional interpretative goal.

Miller puts this well when he says that *discontinuity* is one of the central themes of *Beginnings*: 'The difficult concept of a production or assemblage which is not disorder or heterogeneity, and yet not assimilable to the familiar models of order – organic unity, dialectical progression, or genealogical series – in which origin fathers forth a sequence leading without break to some fore-ordained end'.[8] Instead of these familiar models, which Said would elsewhere call *filiative*, and which might be taken to be comparable to the order of the patriarchal family, he wishes to put forward the idea of an ensemble broken by rifts, lacunae, and differences, 'a sort of multileveled coherence of dispersion', which is kept together all the same by the beginning intention and the method. This means that Said is interested in *Beginnings* in effecting a number of purposes: (1) he wishes to organise his materials in a way that contravenes conventional literary history; (2) he wishes to examine the textual practices implied by such a notion of discontinuity and which he finds, most particularly, in the great works of literary and philosophical modernism; (3) he wishes himself, in his own book, to generate and create such an assemblage of his materials. Said is often accused of a kind of genial liberal eclecticism, but in *Beginnings* we see the founding principle of this openness to the work of others. In this book, and in other much later works such as *Culture and Imperialism*, Said commandeers, appropriates, opens space for, an extraordinarily wide range of other texts, but the point is that he is creating a new kind of order in his disposal and dispersal of these texts.

An author who features prominently in *Beginnings* is the eighteenth-century Irish writer Jonathan Swift. The narrator of Swift's discourse *The Battle of the Books* (a satire on the quarrels in France and England at the end of the seventeenth century about the respective merits of ancient, or classical, and modern knowledge), betrays an attitude where books are seen to rival each other, to seek the monopoly of readerly attention, to seek to push each other aside. To this model of literary production as struggle and contest, Said contrasts Coleridge's welcome for Wordsworth in the poem 'To William Wordsworth', where one poet creates a kind of space for another. In contrast to Swift's model of quarrelsome texts which constantly seek to elbow each other aside, Coleridge presumes that the poem can evoke human presence. Yet in both cases, Said notes, 'writing is a form of displacement'.[9] The relationship of writing to other writing is also one fraught with anxiety, whether that is the anxiety of being late, coming after, being in an inferior position vis-à-vis other writing; or criticism's sense of being perpetually secondary, when, actually, critical writing seeks to understand a literary text better than it does itself.

Said is concerned in *Beginnings* with what he calls the *authority* of writing. Does it reside in the existential writer who wrote? Does it derive from a spirit or *Zeitgeist*? Or does it come from discourse, a wider ensemble of texts that surround the text in question, as Foucault argues? Or from a sense of a text as one of a series of literary-cultural monuments? Said concludes that '[A]uthority is nomadic': 'it is never in the same place, it is never always at the center, nor is it a sort of ontological capacity for originating every instance of sense'. Criticism does not yet possess 'a manageable existential category for writing', such as 'author', 'mind', or '*Zeitgeist*' which can explain how present writing works or where it begins, on the basis of conditions prior to that writing. Writing is such a complex phenomenon that criticism cannot explain why it takes one form over another.[10]

Nevertheless, Said is confident that writing, to a considerable extent, makes its own authority:

> within the discontinuous system of quotation, reference, duplication, parallel, and allusion which makes up writing, authority – or the specific power that makes up a specific act of writing – can be thought of as something whole and as something invented – as something inclusive and made up, if you like, for the occasion.[11]

This means that attributing the power or force of a text to a prior agency or set of circumstances is of limited value. He quotes Joseph Conrad as having written that 'a book is a deed', and 'the writing of it is an enterprise'. Said is suggesting that writing, rather than being a disciplined withdrawal from the world into a realm of aesthetic intellection, is itself a form of action in the world. 'To begin to write, therefore, is to work a set of instruments, to invent a field of play for them, to enable performance.'[12] It is in this sense that Said would suggest that texts are 'worldly'.

So writing, in these formulations, is neither crudely determined by a network of circumstances outside of itself, nor is it merely self-supporting or self-generating. Writers may no longer invoke the Muse as the source of their work, yet we note that that invocation was a sign of a writer re-focussing his or her energies onto the page. The idea of a writing freed of all constraints or anterior influences is a dream, but Said summarises a crucial element of the literary-critical project of his book when he suggests that the classical novel was at once an attempt to dream the dream as embodied in the novelistic hero and a deliberate instrument for 'molesting' or prodding the dream away from its privacy and freedom. In the movement from a dream of pure authority to a jolting molestation that brings writing back to its existence as a text, there is invention.[13]

Further, for Said, the project of the novel form and that of criticism are closely related. He argues that the invention of a field of study, such as that of the novel or English studies, or the invention of methods of study by means of various theories, are all 'inventions of the kind that permit visions within them of pure continuity, progress, activity, and even achievement'. In addition, Said draws analogies between the critic and the novelistic hero: the critic, he says, is 'molested' in the way the fictional hero was. The critic is subject to pressures from adjoining intellectual discourses, from wider social forces, and particularly from the library, 'that special monster of his working reality that tells him of other writers, which secludes writing and thus, in that partial seclusion from violence and disease, stands, at bottom, for writing only'.[14]

In Chapter 3, 'The Novel as Beginning Intention', Said sets out his themes, and illustrates them with a brief though brilliant discussion of Charles Dickens's novel *Great Expectations*. Said begins by arguing that the novel is a literary form designed to permit the portrayal by a writer of social structures and human characters as they develop. 'Character and societies so represented grow and move in the novel because they mirror a process of engenderment or beginning and growth possible and permissible for the mind to imagine.' Therefore novels are artworks that fulfil a crucial human impulse: to add to the world or to plug perceived gaps in reality by creating characters in whom one can believe. Accordingly, Said is led to examine the institution of the novel as 'a kind of appetite that writers develop for modifying reality – as if from the beginning – as a desire to create a new or beginning fictional entity while accepting the consequences of that desire'.[15]

Said's point is that a useful way of understanding the novel form is to see it as embodying a movement between the power of the writer or main character to make a new world, or to forge change, or to create a new narrative, and the resistances to that innovation and effort. Every novelist has to come to terms with both the surge of his or her own creativity and invention, and the constraints placed on that will by various institutions, including most obviously the institution of the novel itself. To describe this situation, Said deploys two terms: *authority* and *molestation*. For authority, Said traces a complex etymology and semantic richness. Authority links writing to power, to the capacity to inspire belief, to the concept of the author as father or ancestor in addition to writer, and, via its Latin root, to increase production, invention, possession, and continuance. He concludes:

> Taken together these meanings are all grounded in the following notions: (1) that of the power of an individual to initiate, institute, establish – in short to begin; (2) that this power and its product are an increase over what had been there previously; (3) that the individual wielding this power controls its issue and what is derived therefrom; (4) that authority maintains the continuity of its course.[16]

Molestation, by contrast, is the name Said gives to the anxieties of this kind of authority. Molestation is the understanding, in an author or a hero, that no matter how apparently complete his or her authority seems, it is never total or seamless, and it is, finally, a pretence. Molestation is what takes place when an author or character is made to realise that he or she is, in fact, sequestered in a realm of mere text, that whatever the effort to create or invent an alternative reality, it is, in the end, an invention which, when compared to empirical reality, will always come up short. Equally, molestation is that disillusionment which has been a major theme of the novel form, all the way from Cervantes's *Don Quixote* through Balzac's *Illusions Perdues*, up to Woolf's *To the Lighthouse*.

Using the work of Søren Kierkegaard, Marx, and Vico, Said sets out three conditions necessary for the generation of novelistic beginnings. The first of these is the sense that the authority of any single voice, or group of voices, is insufficient. In the trio constituted by author, reader, and character, Said suggests, each desires the company of another: 'Each hears in the other the seductive beginning of a new life, an alternative to his own; and yet each grows progressively aware of an authenticity betrayed during the course of the partnership – the novelistic character feels this most of all.'[17] The second condition is that the truth can only be approached obliquely, via a mediation whose manifest falsity throws the truth into relief. The third special condition is the fear of emptiness or nullity that may lie behind or before private authority. By way of illustration of this point, Said points us back to heroes of the early novel, Robinson Crusoe and Tristram Shandy. Both are characters regarding whose origins their respective narratives are obsessed. 'A whole range of principal characters in fiction are based upon the same premise', Said argues: 'orphans, outcasts, parvenus, emanations, solitaries and deranged types whose background is either rejected, mysterious, or unknown.'[18]

The novel, then, is 'a literary form of secondariness', it 'makes, procreates, a certain secondary and alternative life possible for heroes who are otherwise lost in society'. The novelistic institution's attitude to its cast of characters is paternal, that of a father who has given his children a patrimony to which he also is eternally limited. Said then notes that being an author inserts the writer in an extraordinary chain of filiation. He illustrates this with reference to *Don Quixote*:

> There is the Cervantes-Sidi Hamete-Quixote relationship. There is the Amadis-Quixote relationship, there is the astonishingly fertile link between Quixote and Panza – now one, now the other rears his partner in the furthering and fathering forth of illusion; and there is, as every novelist and historian of the novel avers, *Don Quixote* itself as parent novel.[19]

Said wishes to argue that the novelistic character represents and embodies a form of alternative life – humanly invented life – that has its existence in the extraordinary network and heritage that is the novel tradition.

For Said, it is important to note that he has approached a view of novelistic beginnings through the work of philosophers such as Kierkegaard, Vico, and Marx. This leads him to draw comparisons between the matter of beginning in the novel and that in philosophy. The philosopher exists in his work and the novelist in hers in a common way of figuring experience. Philosophical work can share some of the same themes as the novel: 'succession, sequence, derivation, portrayal, and alternation, to say nothing of authority itself'.[20] Adducing Freud, Said moves on to suggest that we create narratives both to forge an alternative reality and to minimise the pain of experience. Yet the drive to narrative is also a repetitive one: it involves the mind traversing terrain it already knows. This is both an affirming and a negative process:

> The novelistic character gains his fictional authority . . . in the desire to escape death; therefore, the narrative process endures so long as that essentially procreative will persists. Yet because a character's real beginning takes place in the avoidance of the anonymity of pure negation . . . there is a simultaneous pressure exerted upon him by that which he is always resisting. The demystification, the decreation or education, of illusions, which is the novel's central theme . . . is thus an enactment of the character's increasing molestation by a truer process pushing him to an ending that resembles his beginning in the midst of negation. The sheer length of the classical novel can almost be accounted for by the desire to initiate and promote a reduplication of life and, at the same time, to allow for a convincing portrayal of how that sort of life leads inevitably to the revelation of a merely borrowed authority.[21]

Said argues that it is crucial to understand narrative 'as wholly qualified by the extremely complex authority of its presentation'.[22] Pip (in *Great Expectations*), Dorothea (in George Eliot's *Middlemarch*), and Isabel (in Henry James's

The Portrait of a Lady), all are characters who suffer from their own illusions. Yet, as Said says, they do *move*, a *beginning* arises out of them. Their mobility is part of their attractiveness or interest as characters. Their kinetic quality is counterpointed in each case with a character marked by stasis. In Pip's case, there is Miss Havisham, who lives frozen in a sort of mausoleum of her own making. In Dorothea's case, there is her first husband, the desiccated and doomed scholar Casaubon, who notoriously announces that he 'lives too much with the dead'. In Isabel's case, there is her husband, Gilbert Osmond, who embodies a life-denying aestheticism.

Pip is a particularly interesting case for Said. He argues that Pip is the condition of being of the novel, its action, and its character. Even his name denotes a beginning as well as an identity, after its abbreviation from Philip Pirrip, the proper name he has by the 'authority' of his parents' tombstone and his sister's order. Pip is, for Said, an alternative being: he is an orphan, the adopted but unwanted surrogate son of a considerably older sister. This pattern is perpetuated throughout the novel. One sees Pip's true background in brief flashes, via Biddy, Joe, and the young Pip who appears at the very end of the novel, even while he is eagerly inventing new genealogies for himself. These begin with the artificial family around Mrs Joe, but recur throughout the novel. Repeatedly, Pip insinuates himself into and then situates himself at the heart of families or family groups. Repeatedly, he challenges their authority on the basis of his 'great expectations', only for the challenge to be undermined by those same expectations, which will eventually break him. Repeatedly, families are shown to be mere elements within older, more powerful familial structures. Miss Havisham's and Estella's arrangement gradually expands to admit Mr Jaggers, then Magwitch, Compeyson, and Molly. Each expansion, each revelation of further 'family' members to Pip shows him to be more compromised, and less central. One might say that Pip's authorising attempts to render himself central are repeatedly molested by forces or circumstances that undercut his sense of himself as a 'gentleman'. Pip learns, in painful increments, more and more about his beginning circumstances, which deflates his sense of himself.

Overall, Dickens parallels Pip's authorising drive to become a gentleman with molesting evidence of his connection with incarceration and criminality. Further, Pip's irrepressible impulse to construe minor events into self-aggrandising structures, as he does with his early visits to Miss Havisham, in the face of Joe's warnings, is mocked and satirised by the comparable but more openly comical constructions of Wemmick and Wopsle. As Said says, these characters are *bricoleurs*, who cobble together their sense of themselves from scattered fragmentary materials, asserting their authority over the threat of being broken up and dispersed. Their comical efforts at self-authorising serve to alert us to the same pattern in Pip.

The basic pattern here is that of life and death. Pip's beginning is the death of his parents. In response to the 'long series of graves and tombstones' that seems to mark the start of his life, Pip creates a path through life for himself, constantly turning from one way to the next as he finds his route blocked. For Said, Pip, like Isabel and Dorothea, 'is conceived as excess': he perpetually wants to be more than he is. His surging will to do more, to become more, is rooted in the deaths from which he emerges and to which he returns at the novel's conclusion.[23]

By the end of the novel, of course, the new Pip has emerged. Said suggests that, between them, 'the two Pips cover an expanse whose poles are true life, on the one hand, and novelistic life, on the other'.[24] The two Pips are Dickens's way of dramatising the molestations of truth over against an overweening authority in need of restraint. That Pip's final molestation, by the appearance of young Pip, comes only at the end of the novel is evidence, in Said's reading, that it was late in his career that Dickens came to see the problem of authority as rooted in the self, and therefore as also to be halted by the self. Young Pip's emergence is a confirmation of Pip's transgressions, and of his alienation from society. In his earlier works, such as *Martin Chuzzlewit*, Dickens had separated the drama of self into two Martins, estranged from each other, who are educated into an embrace. But in later nineteenth-century novels and fictions, the self's authority is divided once again: Said cites Oscar Wilde's *The Picture of Dorian Gray*, Robert Louis Stevenson's *Dr Jekyll and Mr Hyde*, and Conrad's 'The Secret Sharer'. In these narratives, the *alter ego* is a reminder of the instability of the authority of the chief self: 'Jekyll's sense of "the fortress of identity" includes as well a recognition that the fortress has hideous, molesting foundations.'[25] Said notes that the later Dickens did not wish to dramatise that recognition outside of the individual. Pip is both the architect, or author, of his expectations, and their destroyer. There are no excuses or evasions for Pip regarding his responsibility, his choices, his course, his complicities – not in orphanhood or poverty.

Pip's early act of charity under duress – taking a file to Magwitch – is the root of all his later experiences, and also of all his later troubles. It would be too much, according to Said, to see in Pip's actions an aesthetic repetition of the ministry and agony of Christ, and yet the novel form embodies the Christian Western ethos: 'The original instance of divine errancy, the Incarnation, transformed God into man, an alternative being – the record of that mystery is given in language that only approximates the deed.'[26]

For Said, the novel represents a highly mediated and secularised version of that Christian tale:

> The beginning attribution of authority to a character by a
> writer; the implementation of that authority in a narrative form, and the
> burdens and difficulties admitted as a result – all these are ways by which
> the almost numinous communal institutions of language accept and
> conserve the imprint of an individual force. This is why the novel is an
> institutionalisation of the intention to begin. If in the end this institution
> chastens the individual, it is because he needs to be reminded that private
> authority is part of an integral truth that it nevertheless cannot fully
> imitate. The authority of any single piece of fiction repeats that insight,
> for invariably the central consciousness of a novel is found wanting
> in the wholeness which we normally associate with truth. Each piece
> of fiction, therefore, excludes a larger truth than it contains, even though
> it is the novelist's task to make his readers see active relationships among
> various orders of reality or truth both inside and outside the text.[27]

What we take from this is Said's sense that the novel form is the major cultural institution for the creation – or, in Vichian terms, the invention – of the idea of the self. In another sense, though, it also dramatises the crisis of the self, or subject, almost from its inception in the eighteenth century. The self is best understood as located in some familial order, and thus narrative is linked to a biological order. Yet no sooner has the self been invented, one might say, than one realises that its narration is subject to molestations that inhere in it. Novels such as *Great Expectations* or *Tom Jones* are explicitly about this issue. The foundling at the start of *Tom Jones* is then given a clarified paternity by means of the narrative. But with Pip, such comfort does not come, and for Said this is a hint of the problematic of the modernist novel. The move from the classical novel to the modern novel involves the displacement of authority by 'repetition', mimesis or realistic representation is replaced by parody, and innovation changes to rewriting. With modernism, each 'new novel recapitulates not life but other novels'.[28]

As we saw in Chapter Two, Said's account in *Beginnings* of this shift to modernism is illustrated as much by reference to mid twentieth-century critical theory, notably represented by the figure of Michel Foucault, as by discussions of fiction or other literature. In the critical models advanced by Foucault, we find precisely that crisis of authority, mimesis, and innovation described above. In Foucault the problematic of beginnings is subjected to a treatment similar to that which Said delineates in modernist writers such as Proust and T. E. Lawrence.

We can say that in *Beginnings* Said set out for himself both a set of problems –
analysing a writer's career, locating a writer vis-à-vis a tradition, studying
how a writer initiates a career or a project, tracking these issues across the
crucial transition from nineteenth-century post-Enlightenment intellectual
and aesthetic confidence to fin-de-siècle narrative and representational crisis
and authorial anxiety – and also developed a series of tools and concepts –
authority and its molesting discontents, the idea of a secular worldly beginning
as against a transcendent or ahistorical origin, the historicism of Vico – which
he would deploy repeatedly over the rest of his career. *Beginnings* is in part a
book about writerly careers, and the forces that impede them (not least the
effects of writing itself), but it is also a deliberate career-launching gambit on
Said's own part.

Orientalism (1978)

Beginnings, as we have seen, is, among many other things, a complex and rich
'beginning' itself: 'To begin to write, therefore, is to work a set of instruments, to
invent a field of play for them, to enable performance.'[29] *Orientalism*, published
in 1978, but already extensively thought out and planned by 1975, takes some
of the instruments of *Beginnings*, and redeploys them in a new field of play. Yet
Orientalism has been by far the most acclaimed and influential of these two
books.

Beginnings was respectfully received. Its particular conjugation of theoretical, methodological, and literary-critical interests and themes interested and
intrigued some readers, and baffled others. But it has been that book's fate to be
overshadowed and to a great degree occluded by *Orientalism*, which so swiftly
followed it. Said himself, writing about the latter book in 1995, described
it as having become 'in almost a Borgesian way . . . several different books'.[30]
By this, he suggests his veritable bewilderment at the extraordinary global
phenomenon that *Orientalism* – which was translated into at least seventeen
languages – had become.

So, then, what is Orientalism? Said offers several overlapping answers to this
basic question. It is, first of all, 'a way of coming to terms with the Orient that
is based on the Orient's special place in the European Western experience'. But
more formally, for Said, it encompasses three aspects or elements:

(1) it is an academic field. 'Anyone who teaches, writes about, or researches
    the Orient – and this applies whether the person is an anthropologist,

sociologist, historian or philologist – either in its specific or its general aspects, is an Orientalist, and what he or she does is Orientalism';

(2) at a broader but also deeper level, 'Orientalism is a style of thought based upon an ontological and epistemological distinction made between the "Orient" and (most of the time) the "Occident"';

(3) in a manner that relates to the two definitions above, it is also an institution of domination: 'Taking the late eighteenth century as a very roughly defined starting point Orientalism can be discussed and analyzed as the corporate institution for dealing with the Orient – dealing with it by making statements about it, authorizing views of it, describing it, by teaching it, settling it, ruling over it; in short, Orientalism as a Western style for dominating, restructuring and having authority over the Orient'.[31]

The point here is that Said is, firstly, making an intervention into, and a critique of, an academic field and tradition: that of the study of the Orient. But, secondly, when he invokes Orientalism as a 'style of thought', he is suggesting that this 'ontological and epistemological distinction' between Orient and Occident, between East and West, can be traced far more widely than just in an academic speciality. Thirdly, implicitly, Said is linking the production of academic knowledge about the Orient, and that much wider trope of the dividing line between East and West, to 'the corporate institution for . . . having authority over the Orient'. That is, we will find him suggesting that academic writing, and all sorts of other writing about the Orient also – that of travellers, colonial administrators and soldiers, missionaries, poets, philosophers, economists – has been related to the exercise of power and authority in the Orient.

Said deals principally with British and French, and latterly American, Orientalism. That he does not deal with the large mass of writing produced about the Orient by other European intellectual traditions has been a matter of criticism. Said argues that the British and French experience of the Orient is particular: 'Orientalism derives from a particular closeness experienced between Britain and France and the Orient.'[32] Accordingly, Orientalism is a 'cultural enterprise' which encompasses areas and matters as diverse as the spice trade, the Biblical texts and the Biblical lands, Oriental 'experts' and 'old hands', and imaginative tropes such as Oriental sensuality, irrationality, violence, spirituality. Furthermore, this enterprise is one that, since 1945, has been inherited by the United States in its relations with the Orient.

'The Orient', therefore, is not merely a physical region; rather the very concept of that region is, for Said, a cultural construction. The Orient's status as a region does not originate in specific geophysical characteristics, or homo-geneities of culture or society or history. Rather, 'the Orient' is a concept that has acquired a history and tradition of ideas, metaphors, terminology, which have been the means by which the Orient has been represented, made real, to the West.

Said's interest is not in the Orient, in any empirical sense. His work is not intended as a defence of the Orient from Western misrepresentation. About the reality of the countries and peoples of the Orient, his 'study of Orientalism has very little to contribute, except to acknowledge it, tacitly'. The point, rather, is that he is less interested in any relationship between Orientalism and its object than in 'the internal consistency of Orientalism and its ideas about the Orient . . . despite or beyond any correspondence, or lack thereof, with a "real" Orient'.[33]

Orientalism, accordingly, is *not* a book about Islam, or Arab history or culture, or the peoples, societies, economies, or political systems of the Orient. It *is* about the body of writing about or concerning the Orient, by Westerners, and the density, texture, structures, patterns, and variations of that writing. Said stresses that the relationship between the West and the Orient has been one of *power*. The Orient has been 'Orientalised' or described as 'Oriental' not merely because it has displayed the characteristics Westerners associate with 'the Oriental', *but because it could be*. The point is that this imbalance of power is discernible in *writing*. Orientalism is not, for Said, merely a set of elaborate lies or myths that can simply be punctured or corrected. Orientalism is not simply *wrong* (though of course it can be that). While he believed that Orientalism was less a 'veridic discourse' on the Orient than an expression of power over it, he is not interested in a merely moral critique:

> what we must respect and try to grasp is the sheer knitted-together strength of Orientalist discourse, its very close ties to the enabling socio-economic and political institutions, and its redoubtable durability.[34]

What is important about Orientalism, then, is its quasi-material density and *persistence*, and its capacity thereby to monopolise the field of representation of the Oriental.

At this point, we must note Said's appropriation of Foucault in *Orientalism*, one of the more controversial aspects of the book. Said is interested in constru-ing Orientalism as a *discourse*. For Foucault, a discourse is a body of statements – spoken and written in language, though discourse can also encompass other forms of representation – that can be, and are, made about a specific matter. Authoritative discourses acquire, by means of their links to institutions such as the legal system, the state, the academy, and the sciences, the status of 'truth'. Foucault called this nexus *power/knowledge* – in this formulation, knowledge, or truth-statement, is a form of power, and, equally, power can be understood in its capacity to produce effects or 'regimes' of truth. Famously, in books such as *History of Madness*, *The Birth of the Clinic*, and *Discipline and Punish*, Foucault looked at how, in European societies, modes of knowledge-production such as the asylum and psychiatry, medicine and the hospital, and penology and the prison, create bodies of information and codes of practice that purport to offer 'truthful' statements about their objects – the insane, the sick, and the criminal – but which are also modes of linguistic construction and determination of those objects.

Treating Orientalism as a discourse allows Said to argue that it can be understood as 'the enormously systematic discipline by which European culture was able to manage – and even produce – the Orient politically, sociologically, militarily, ideologically, scientifically, and imaginatively during the post-Enlightenment period'.[35] Such was the strength of this discourse that no-one writing about, acting in, or thinking about the Orient could avoid its capture. The grasp of the discourse, however, is not, for Said, complete: it does not simply determine 'what can be said about the Orient, but . . . it is the whole network of interests inevitably brought to bear on (and therefore always involved in) any occasion when that peculiar entity the "Orient" is in question'.[36]

Yet at least as strong as the influence of Foucault in *Orientalism* is that of Gramsci. The Italian Marxist's conception of *hegemony* is crucial to Said's argument about the relationship of intellectual or artistic work, and the raw political and material facts of Western dominance of the Orient. Starting from Gramsci's separation of political society from civil society, Said does not argue that Orientalism is a crude reflection of political interests, nor that it is simply wrong, nor that it is a grandly orchestrated ideological conspiracy for Western 'control' of the Orient. Rather, though it is produced in the realm of civil society – in universities, learned societies, academic journals, foreign policy think-tanks, by poets and writers, anthropologists and philologists – it is nevertheless usefully affiliated with elements of political society. As we saw in Chapter Two, Said argues that Orientalism is a part of and contributory to Western *hegemony*. Hegemony, for Gramsci, is ideological leadership, or the capacity of a set of ideas to win the consent of a social group or class. Hegemonic ideas are those that are widely diffused in a society, and that attain authoritative status. Hegemonic ideas are those which, though they emanate from authority, have been so introjected by a wider audience as to seem to represent that audience's own ideas and deepest feelings. The hegemony of

Orientalist understanding of the Orient is created by the relationship of those civic organisations with the directly political forces of the government and the state. Therefore, Orientalism is

> a *distribution* of geopolitical awareness into aesthetic, scholarly, economic, sociological, historical and philological texts; it is an *elaboration* not only of a basic geographical distinction (the world is made up of two unequal halves, Orient and Occident) but also of a whole series of 'interests' which, by such means as scholarly discovery, philological reconstruction, psychological analysis, landscape and sociological description, it not only creates but maintains; it *is*, rather than expresses, a certain *will* or *intention* to understand, in some cases to control, manipulate, even to incorporate, what is a manifestly different (or alternative and novel) world.

Said's argument here is that Orientalism is a cultural-intellectual field and activity that is suffused with a geopolitical sense, a realm of discourse where that geopolitical sense – the sense of geographical distinction, the sense of bearing or containing 'interests' – has become hegemonic, a background assumption. Not merely this, but it has become, however obliquely, itself the desire and effort to incorporate the non-Western world.

> [I]t is, above all, a discourse that is by no means in direct, corresponding relationship with political power in the raw, but rather is produced and exists in an uneven exchange with various kinds of power, shaped to a degree by the exchange with power political (as with a colonial or imperial establishment), power intellectual (as with reigning sciences like comparative linguistics or anatomy, or any of the modern policy sciences), power cultural (as with orthodoxies and canons of taste, texts, values), power moral (as with ideas about what 'we' do and what 'they' cannot do or understand as 'we' do).[37]

Orientalist knowledge, then, is produced in proximity to power, and is itself soaked with various kinds and gradations of power. Yet to say this is not merely to denigrate such knowledge or such cultural-intellectual activity. In a related way, Said's argument is not that the regularities and codes of Orientalism have crudely inhibited those who wrote or write about the Orient. On the contrary, the power of the discourse lies in the way it supports, affirms, and offers possibilities to a writer. Gramsci and Foucault, for all their differences, both suggest that power is productive; that the persistence and durability of hegemonic systems lies not in their coercive strength, but in the richness and variety of elaborations on directive thought that they make possible.

Having argued that Orientalism is a discourse produced in a specific relation to power, Said wishes at the same time to note that that relationship does not exhaust the discourse or its interest. A wide variety of questions must also be posed to Orientalism:

> What other sorts of intellectual, aesthetic, scholarly and cultural energies went into the making of an imperialist tradition like the Orientalist one? How did philology, lexicography, history, biology, political and economic theory, novel-writing and lyric poetry come to the service of Orientalism's broadly imperialist view of the world? What changes, modulations, refinements, even revolutions take place within Orientalism? What is the meaning of originality, of continuity, of individuality, in this context? How does Orientalism transmit or reproduce itself from one epoch to another? In fine, how can we treat the cultural, historical phenomenon of Orientalism as a kind of *willed human work* . . . in all its historical complexity, detail and worth without at the same time losing sight of the alliance between cultural work, political tendencies, the state and the specific realities of domination?[38]

Several elements in this passage merit discussion. Firstly, we see how Said is suggesting that Orientalism is internally extremely various and rich, containing multiple ideas, practices, and intellectual and cultural forms. Secondly, and conversely, we see that he is suggesting that all of these nevertheless feed into 'a broadly imperialist tradition'. Thirdly, he is suggesting that Orientalism should not be seen as a 'reflection' of an imperialist tradition, or as somehow 'caused by' the practices and history of empire. Orientalism is not a secondary or anterior phenomenon. Rather, Orientalism, in Said's sense, *is* the tradition. Orientalism is an inherent, equal, and significant part of the imperialist tradition.

We should also note in this passage the echoes of *Beginnings*. We hear these echoes in the question about the changes and modulations in Orientalism. We hear them in the question about Orientalism's capacity for self-transmission and reproduction. We hear them more insistently in the question about the 'meaning of originality, of continuity, of individuality' in Orientalism, and in the idea of Orientalism as 'willed human work'. Clearly, Said's conceptualisation of Orientalism is one derived in part from his ideas of beginnings.

Accordingly, it is not surprising to find that *Orientalism* returns to the theme of beginnings itself, although it does so in terms less abstract or literary than *Beginnings*. '[B]eginnings have to be made for each project in such a way as to *enable* what follows from them', Said announces. However, designating a beginning in this situation is peculiarly difficult. It involves 'an act of delimitation', by which the material to be worked upon is separated out from a much larger mass, and is designated a beginning. Working with Orientalism necessitates not only finding a point of departure, but also choosing which texts, authors, and periods are the best ones to be studied.[39]

The problems that Said identifies concerning his own intervention into Orientalism are multiple. He eschews a grand historical narrative of the history and development of Orientalism as a potentially limitless project, but also points out that a narrative history is not what he is interested in, and other books already fulfil this purpose. He admits that his work does not do justice to the contributions of European cultures other than the British and the French to Orientalism, yet he maintains that the sheer quality of British, French, and, later, American, scholarship lifts it above the rest. In particular, he admits his lack of coverage of German Orientalism is problematic. 'Any work that seeks to provide an understanding of academic Orientalism and pays little attention to scholars like Steinthal, Müller, Becker, Goldziher, Brockelmann, Noldeke – to mention only a handful – needs reproaching, and I freely reproach myself.'[40] Said acknowledges the immense prestige that had been won by German Romance scholarship by 1830, but he also reminds us that at no point in the first two-thirds of the nineteenth century was there a substantial German presence in the Orient. Germany had no national interest in the Orient – of course this is largely because Germany was not a nation-state until 1871.

Said stresses two methodological themes, initially. The first of these is *authority*, which is a term taken over directly from *Beginnings*. In the earlier book, authority was discussed as an attribute of authors and characters who provide novels with their self-creating drive. In *Orientalism* it is discussed in rather more materialist terms:

> There is nothing mysterious or natural about authority. It is formed, irradiated, disseminated; it is instrumental, it is persuasive; it has status, it establishes canons of taste and value; it is virtually indistinguishable from certain ideas it dignifies as true, and from traditions, perceptions, and judgements it forms, transmits, reproduces. Above all, authority can, indeed must, be analyzed. All these attributes of authority apply to Orientalism, and much of what I do in this study is to describe both the historical authority in and the personal authorities of Orientalism.[41]

Said suggests two terms with which to study authority. These are *strategic location* and *strategic formation*. An author's strategic location for Said is that author's position in his text regarding the Oriental material he writes about. A strategic formation is a name for the relations between texts, 'the way in which groups of texts, types of texts, even textual genres, acquire mass, density, and referential power among themselves and thereafter in the culture at large'.[42] By this Said is referring to the way that texts can acquire a kind of worldly value, force, and effect – in short, how they come to be or to create hegemony. Every writer confronting the Orient must come up with various kinds of textual and narrative procedures to allow himself not to be overwhelmed by the material. This act of authorial self-positioning includes the matter of narrative voice and tone, the structure or pattern used to organise the material, the 'images, themes, motifs that circulate in his text' – in short, the textual strategies and rhetorical modes the author uses to address the reader, to grasp the Orient, and to authorise himself to speak about it and represent it. Furthermore, texts locate themselves in a tradition, posit relationships with other texts, and thereby assemble themselves into the kinds of analysable formations to which Said refers. The affiliations that texts accumulate in this manner are part also of what creates their authority.[43]

The second methodological theme Said prioritises is *exteriority*. By this term he refers to his interest not in ideas hidden in the Orientalist text, but in its *surface*. For Said, Orientalism assumes exteriority: the Orientalist author is always outside of his Oriental material or subject, and his text is designed to demonstrate that separateness. This exteriority allows the Orientalist author to represent the Orient to his reader, to speak for the Orient, to bring it to life for the reader, to animate it, to explain it to the Western reader. Orientalist texts are *representations*; it is a frequent assumption of Orientalist texts that the author is representing an Orient that is not capable of representing itself: hence Said's quotation from Marx's *Eighteenth Brumaire of Louis Bonaparte* in one of the epigraphs for the book: 'They cannot represent themselves; they must be represented.' Said stresses that what interests him is not the truth value of Orientalism, but the literary-rhetorical aspects of the discourse: its styles, its figures of speech, its settings, its narrative techniques. It is these, not the 'presence' of the Orient in Orientalist writings, that need to be studied. Just as he stressed in *Beginnings* that 'writing is a form of displacement', so Said is suggesting that writing about the Orient has very little to do with telling 'the truth'; rather, in fact, writing attains the condition of a presence to the reader precisely by having displaced the empirical world:

> Thus all of Orientalism stands forth and away from the Orient: that Orientalism makes sense at all depends more on the West than on the Orient, and this sense is directly indebted to various Western techniques of representation that make the Orient visible, clear, 'there' in discourse about it.[44]

However, Said also wishes to stress that his book is not an exercise in the history of ideas, conventionally conceived. Orientalist writings – from philological treatises to Romantic travel narratives to policy reports – do not exist in a realm of pure ideality. Rather, and in this Said is following Foucault, the point of Orientalism is to argue that these ideas, these texts, this discourse possess a weight and force, an effectiveness, a durability and worldly presence of their own.

Said deviates from Foucault in respect of the relationship of individual authors to the discourse. For Foucault, a discourse is a system of linguistic rules and protocols that govern what it is possible to say or write in a specific field. The individual author, for Foucault, will always be subsumed within this wider system: his or her work will always be shaped, channelled, and finally restricted by the order of discourse. But Said declares that he does believe 'in the determining imprint of individual authors upon the otherwise anonymous collective body of texts constituting a discursive formation like Orientalism'.[45] For example, great nineteenth-century writers such as Gérard de Nerval, Gustave Flaubert, and Richard Burton all read and cited the work of Edward Lane. Lane's works lent their authority to those who learned from him and came after him. In this way his work became more than itself: in Said's words, it acquired 'mass, density, and referential power'. Yet Lane's own personal style was important, and contributed to his very currency.

Said also stresses the personal aspect to his writing of *Orientalism*. This is a way that his ideas about beginnings can be seen to have implications for an individual writer, and in fact for the theorist of beginnings himself. Nonetheless, as with the use of the idea of authority, we find here the notion of beginning is given a much more explicitly material and socio-historical inflection than was the case in *Beginnings*. Said quotes Gramsci:

> The starting point of critical elaboration is the consciousness of what one really is, and is 'knowing thyself' as a product of the historical process to date, which has deposited in you an infinity of traces, without leaving an inventory . . . therefore it is imperative at the outset to compile such an inventory.[46]

Therefore, the study of Orientalism is in part, for Said, the making of a personal inventory of the traces left in him by history. He feels himself intensely to be an 'Oriental', but one born in a British Mandate territory and educated in predominantly Western institutions of learning. Even more pressing is his sense of Palestinian identity, which conflicts with the broad Western liberal intellectual consensus of sympathy with Zionism. Politically, Palestinians barely exist, and when they are held to exist, it is only as Orientals, or terrorists, or as an irritant. The Palestinian in America, Said suggests, is subject to a focus of knowledge and power that constructs him as an 'Oriental', but erases him as a human being.

Orientalism is divided into three major chapters, with twelve subdivisions. 'The Scope of Orientalism', the first chapter, sets out a broad overview of Orientalism, with a focus on the issue of representation and certain typical tropes, such as those of Oriental cruelty, Oriental splendour, and Oriental despotism. The second major chapter is entitled 'Oriental Structures and Restructures', and it is concerned with the rise of the institutions of Orientalism – its development as an academic discipline, its founding fathers, its learned societies, and its relationship to the rise of European empire, from the late eighteenth century to the late nineteenth century. The third chapter, 'Orientalism Now', maps the development of Orientalism against the shift of power between the great European colonial empires and the United States.

Though he notes early landmarks of European proto-Orientalist scholarship, such as Barthélemy d'Herbelot's *Bibliothèque Orientale* (1697), Said dates the rise of modern Orientalism to the French invasion of Egypt in 1798. Napoleon Bonaparte was fascinated by Egypt for many reasons. Capturing it would be a useful way of harassing the British, by interposing a French presence between them and their crucial colonial territory in India. But Bonaparte was not moved by merely strategic interests. He had a keen sense of the historical antecedents to his conquest of Egypt, going all the way back to Alexander the Great. Further, his sense of this historical background was one derived from texts: 'he saw the Orient only as it had been encoded first by classical texts and then by Orientalist experts, whose vision, based on classical texts, seemed a useful substitute for any actual encounter with the real Orient'.[47] Bonaparte was influenced by the work of the Comte de Volney, a traveller who published his *Voyage en Egypte et en Syrie* in 1783, and his *Considérations sur la guerre actuel de Turcs* in 1788. Bonaparte cites Volney directly in his own *Campagnes d'Egypte et de Syrie*, dictated during his exile on St Helena. Volney suggested that any French conquest of the Orient would actually involve three wars: one against the Ottoman *porte*; another against Britain; and yet a third against Islam. Yet Napoleon tried everywhere to persuade Egyptians that he was *for* Islam. Every ordinance was translated into Koranic Arabic, and the imperial army was enjoined always to respect Islamic sensibilities. When he realised that his army was too small simply to conquer Egypt, Bonaparte recruited the local Muslim clergy to interpret the Koran in terms favourable to the Grande Armée, conferring military honours on them, and impressing them with his own knowledge of the text.

An *école publique* in the languages of Arabic, Turkish, and Persian had been established in Paris by revolutionary decree in 1793. Its first teacher of

Arabic was Sylvestre de Sacy, the first great academic Orientalist: many of Napoleon's translators were students of Sacy's, and his influence dominated European Orientalism for decades to come. The conquest of Egypt was as much a textual matter as one of military power. The result was the mighty *Description de l'Egypte*, published in twenty-three volumes between 1809 and 1828. The purpose and effect of the *Description* is rendered by Said in one notable sentence, whose accumulating momentum and power dramatise the authority of the discourse he is trying to describe:

> To restore a region from its present barbarism to its former classical greatness; to instruct (for its own benefit) the Orient in the ways of the modern West; to subordinate or underplay military power in order to aggrandize the project of glorious knowledge acquired in the process of political domination of the Orient; to formulate the Orient, to give it shape, identity, definition with full recognition of its place in memory, its importance to imperial strategy, and its 'natural' role as an appendage to Europe; to dignify all the knowledge collected during colonial occupation with the title 'contribution to modern learning' when the natives had neither been consulted nor treated as anything except as pretexts for a text whose usefulness was not to the natives; to feel oneself as a European in command, almost at will, of Oriental history, time and geography; to institute new areas of specialization; to establish new disciplines; to divide, deploy, schematize, tabulate, index and record everything in sight (and out of sight); to make out of every observable detail a generalization and out of every generalization an immutable law about the Oriental nature, temperament, mentality, custom or type; and, above all, to transmute living reality into the stuff of texts, to possess (and think one possesses) actuality mainly because nothing in the Orient seems to resist one's powers: these are the features of Orientalist projection entirely realized in the *Description de l'Egypte*, itself enabled and reinforced by Napoleon's wholly Orientalist engulfment of Egypt by the instruments of Western knowledge and power.[48]

Such was the astonishing ambition and power of this project that, notwith-standing the short duration of the Napoleonic occupation of Egypt, its cultural and intellectual legacy was enormous: 'Quite literally, the occupation gave birth to the entire modern experience of the Orient as interpreted from within the universe of discourse founded by Napoleon in Egypt, whose agencies of domination and dissemination included the Institut and the *Description*.' Said identifies such classics of nineteenth-century literature as the Vicomte de Chateaubriand's *Itinéraire de Paris à Jérusalem, et de Jérusalem à Paris* (1810– 11), Alphonse de Lamartine's *Voyage en Orient* (1835), Gustave Flaubert's

Salammbô (1862), Edward Lane's *Manners and Customs of the Modern Egyptians* (1836), and Richard Burton's *Personal Narrative of a Pilgrimage to al-Madinah and Meccah* (1855) as 'textual children' of the *Description*.[49] But further, the philological work of Ernest Renan, especially his *Système comparé et histoire générale des langues sémitiques* (1848) and even geopolitical projects, such as Ferdinand de Lesseps's Suez Canal and Britain's occupation of Egypt in 1882, are reckoned by Said to flow from the Napoleonic occupation, military and discursive.

Said notes the relationship between the rise of Orientalism and crucial European intellectual currents of the late eighteenth and early nineteenth centuries. The great discoveries at the start of Romance philology, and the Romantic movement more broadly, were intimately related to Orientalism. The modern European study of comparative linguistics owes its origins to Romantic thinkers such as Johann Gottfried Herder, but also to discoveries regarding Oriental languages by William Jones, Franz Bopp, Jakob Grimm, and others, who studied Oriental texts brought to Paris and London. Comparative philology was predicated at this time on the idea of families of languages, of which two of the chiefs were the Semitic languages and the Indo-European languages. Said argues that from the start,

> Orientalism carried forward two traits: (1) a newly found scientific
> self-consciousness based on the linguistic importance of the Orient to
> Europe, and (2) a proclivity to divide, subdivide, and redivide its subject
> matter without ever changing its mind about the Orient as being always
> the same, unchanging, uniform, and radically peculiar object.[50]

Accordingly, the German Romantic writer Friedrich Schlegel, in his *Über die Sprache und Weisheit der Indier* (1808), reckoned that Sanskrit and Persian, and German and Greek, were more closely related to each other than to Semitic or African languages. The Indo-European languages were 'artistically simple and satisfactory' where the Semitic languages were not. The latter were, in Said's gloss on Schlegel, 'agglutinative, unaesthetic, and mechanical'; they were 'different, inferior, backward'.[51] Said points out that for Schlegel and other Romantics, the cultural richness of the Orient was discernible only in its 'classical' past, not in its debased present. What interests Said here is how distinctions made between *languages* were generalised out onto *cultures and peoples*, and that this moved inevitably towards hierarchical views of cultures and peoples. This is a trend that was to be found in other Romantic thinkers, such as Herder, Grimm, and, much more obviously, Johann Gottlieb Fichte. Starting from these origins in philology, Said suggests that the 'official genealogy of Orientalism' would include and suffuse much of the intellectual life and community of nineteenth-century Europe. These writers and intellectuals both contributed to, and were shaped by, the discourse of Orientalism that Said seeks to describe.

In 'The Scope of Orientalism', Said sets out the exemplary cases of Arthur James Balfour and Lord Cromer. Balfour was Prime Minster of Great Britain at the start of the twentieth century. Later he was Foreign Secretary and wrote the famous Balfour Declaration, a letter to the Zionist movement in 1917, committing Britain to the creation of a Jewish national home in Palestine. Said, however, quotes a speech Balfour delivered in the House of Commons in 1910. During a debate on the British presence in Egypt, Balfour responds to a question by J. M. Robertson MP, who had asked 'What right have you to take up these airs of superiority with regard to people whom you choose to call Oriental?' His answer to Robertson embodies and dramatises Said's ideas of Orientalism neatly.

Balfour declares that he takes up no air of superiority regarding Egypt and the Egyptians. And yet, '[W]e know the civilization of Egypt better than we know the civilization of any other country'.[52] Balfour is justifying British involvement in Egypt on the basis of knowledge. Knowledge here means a number of things. It means knowing a civilisation from its beginning to its decline. It means being able to transcend the known object. It also means that the object – here, Egypt – is open to the gaze of Western knowledge. Such knowledge is itself a form of authority. 'British knowledge of Egypt is Egypt for Balfour', Said argues, 'and the burdens of knowledge make such questions as inferiority and superiority seem petty ones'.[53] Yet Balfour nowhere denies British superiority or Egyptian inferiority; he assumes them:

> First of all, look at the facts of the case. Western nations as soon as they
> emerge into history show the beginnings of those capacities for
> self-government . . . having merits of their own . . . You may look
> through the whole history of the Orientals in what is called, broadly
> speaking, the East, and you never find traces of self-government.

It is to the benefit of the Orientals that they should now receive this absolute government from Britain. It is good for them, it is good for Britain, and, in fact, it is good for humanity as a whole: 'We are in Egypt not merely for the sake of the Egyptians, though we are there for their sake; we are there also for the sake of Europe at large.'[54]

Balfour does not feel compelled to argue that the Egyptians appreciate or are even aware of the awe-inspiring duty which Britain is carrying out in its rule of Egypt. Balfour makes no reference to Egyptian opinion, the implication being that no Egyptians could hold opinions on their country's governance worth attending to. Britain sends its finest people to work in the grand task of colonial governance, and it is crucial – in the context of the House of Commons debate to which Balfour is contributing – that those colonial officials not be undermined at home. It is crucial, again, not only for the British Empire, but in fact for the Egyptian subjects of the Empire:

> directly the native populations have that instinctive feeling that those with whom they have got to deal have not got behind them . . . the full and ungrudging support of the country which sent them there, those populations lose all that sense of order which is the very basis of their civilization, just as our officers lose all that sense of power and authority, which is the very basis of everything they can do for the benefit of those among whom they have been sent.[55]

Said's argument is that Balfour's thinking has a circular self-confirming logic: 'England knows Egypt; Egypt is what England knows; England knows that Egypt cannot have self-government; England confirms that by occupying Egypt; for the Egyptians, Egypt is what England has occupied and now governs; foreign occupation therefore becomes "the very basis" of contemporary Egyptian civilization; Egypt requires, indeed insists upon, British occupation.'[56]

In the Commons on 30 July 1907, Balfour had advocated the presentation of a retirement prize to Evelyn Baring, Lord Cromer, British governor of Egypt between 1882 (when Britain occupied Egypt) and 1907. Cromer's ideas about Orientals are those of one directly involved in their governance, and so are somewhat cruder than those of Balfour. In January 1908, in the *Edinburgh Review*, Cromer published a long essay on 'subject races'. Cromer argues that the empire is best governed if such things as militarism at home, and 'free institutions' in the foreign territories, are kept to a minimum. Imposing a supposedly scientific mode of rule upon the native is a counterproductive exercise, as logic is something 'the existence of which the Oriental is disposed altogether to ignore'. Rather, the British should accept and understand the native's limitations, and 'endeavour to find, in the contentment of the subject race, a more worthy and, it may be hoped, a stronger bond of union between the rulers and the ruled'.[57] Indians, Egyptians, and Zulus are all '*in statu pupillari*' – students – in terms of nationhood, and therefore their best interests are actually most effectively decided by Britain. If this approach is taken in the British colonies, then 'we may perhaps foster some sort of cosmopolitan allegiance grounded on the respect always accorded to superior talents and unselfish conduct, and on the gratitude derived both from favours conferred and from those to come'. Cromer was resolutely opposed to Egyptian self-determination:

'The real future of Egypt . . . lies not in the direction of a narrow nationalism, which will only embrace native Egyptians . . . but rather in that of an enlarged cosmopolitanism.'[58]

Said argues that the core of Cromer's (and Balfour's) view of Orientals, a view informed by a century of Orientalist learning, lies in the idea that they are 'for all intents and purposes a Platonic essence, which any Orientalist (or ruler of Orientals) might examine, understand and expose'.[59] Said quotes from Cromer's *Modern Egypt*: 'Want of accuracy, which easily degenerates into untruthfulness, is in fact the main characteristic of the Oriental mind.'[60]

Cromer here displays two related tendencies Said considers to be particularly typical of Orientalism: the suggestion that there is an 'Oriental mind' (or spirit or essence), which is common to all Orientals, and which is unchanging over history or geography; and the notion that this Oriental mind is fundamentally irrational. 'The European is a close reasoner', Cromer says. 'He is a natural logician.' But 'the mind of the Oriental . . . like his picturesque streets, is eminently wanting in symmetry. His reasoning is of the most slipshod description.' Arabs are 'singularly deficient in the logical faculty'. Orientals are inveterate liars, they are 'devoid of energy and initiative', 'lethargic and suspicious'.[61] They are, for Cromer, the antithesis of the English.

Said points out that the views expressed by Balfour and Cromer are charac- terised by certain themes and regularities. The Oriental – though Said's focus is the Muslim Middle East, this was said of Asian peoples more widely also – is, most of all, irrational. The Orient and the Oriental have fallen from a long- past civilisational glory, and so they are, in a sense, decadent. The Oriental is also childlike, or essentially feminine, and hence, in patriarchal Victorian English thinking, incapable of self-governance or self-knowledge. By con- trast, the European sets the norm, is rational, self-possessed, self-determining, mature, masculine. Accordingly, the Orient beseeches Western governance, and the Oriental requires Western tutelage and discipline. Yet this thinking goes further, for the suggestion is that the gulf between East and West is so fundamental as to imply that the Oriental has his own social, cultural, even epistemological world, with its own rules and guidelines. But simultaneously, the Oriental's world is given its integrity and definition by the way it is described in Western knowledge. In Said's words,

> Knowledge of the Orient, because generated out of strength, in a sense
> *creates* the Orient, the Oriental, and his world. In Cromer's and Balfour's
> language, the Oriental is depicted as something one judges (as in a
> court of law), something one studies and depicts (as in a curriculum),
> something one disciplines (as in a school or prison), something one

illustrates (as in a zoological manual). The point is that in each of
these cases the Oriental is *contained* and *represented* by dominating
frameworks.[62]

In every sense, the Orient and the Oriental are objects known, analysed,
deployed, and finally commanded by the authorised Western subject.

Said tells us that Orientalist ideas took a wide variety of forms in the nineteenth and twentieth centuries. Contemporaneously with European Roman-
ticism, at the end of the eighteenth century and in the early decades of the
nineteenth century, there was an 'Oriental Renaissance'. At this time, a new
interest in the Orient, here widely defined to include all regions between the
Mediterranean and China, claimed the attention of European scholars, but also
of writers, artists, and politicians. This burgeoning interest was in part caused
by the availability of newly translated texts from the Oriental languages –
Sanskrit, Zend, and Arabic – and also by the inauguration of a new European relationship with the Orient embodied in the Napoleonic conquest of
Egypt in 1798. The subject of Orientalism acquired ever-greater prestige during the nineteenth century. This was the moment of its institutionalisation in
Europe, in the form of chairs of Oriental studies at European universities, and
embodied in organisations such as the Société asiatique, the Royal Asiatic Society, the Deutsche Morgenländische Gesellschaft, and the American Oriental
Society.

Paradoxically, alongside this expanding interest in the Orient went an atten-
uation of what even the most imaginative or radical writers could say about the
Orient. 'Orientalism was ultimately a political vision of reality whose structure
promoted the difference between the familiar (Europe, the West, "us") and
the strange (the Orient, the East, "them").'[63] This vision invented and then
maintained the two spheres. Reality seemed only to reinforce the vision, which
was then further elaborated so as to shape the reality. The Westerner – soldier,
politician, scholar, traveller – always had 'a freedom of intercourse' vis-à-vis
the Orient. Because he came from the stronger culture, he could penetrate,
see, know, and give shape to the Orient and its mysteries. But this strength did
not necessarily confer on the Westerner a great breadth of vision, sympathy, or
understanding of the Orient.

In an essay of Cromer's entitled 'The Government of Subject Races',
Said reads a model for the working of Orientalism. Cromer, writing about
how Britain should administer a far-flung empire, discusses the relationship between local imperial operatives, possessed of detailed specific knowledge derived from the day-to-day contingencies of government, and a central
authority in Britain:

> Cromer envisions a seat of power in the West, and radiating out from it towards the East a great embracing machine, sustaining the central authority yet commanded by it. What the machine's branches feed into it in the East – human material, material wealth, knowledge, what have you – is processed by the machine, then converted into more power. The specialist does the immediate translation of mere Oriental matter into useful substance: the Oriental becomes, for example, a subject race, an example of an 'Oriental' mentality, all for the enhancement of the 'authority' at home.[64]

This image of the self-aggrandising discursive workings of Orientalism is one that will recur in Said's much later book, *Culture and Imperialism*. Orientalism is seen here to be the discursive mechanism by which the West produced and reproduced its authority over the Orient. The concept of authority as formulated in *Beginnings* has here been embodied, dramatised, and institutionalised, but it is still worked out in writing and the production of knowledge.

To illustrate the narrowness of view that the discourse of Orientalism offers to even the most radical writer, Said's reading of Karl Marx is useful. Marx identified his idea of the 'Asiatic mode of production' in 1853, in a series of analyses of British rule in India. What interests Said is the split in Marx between admiration for Britain's revolutionising of socio-economic relations in India, and his human sympathy for the Indian natives caught up in this deracinating, impoverishing, often violent process. Said identifies Marx's conception of the Orient as derived from the Romantic German writer Johann Wolfgang von Goethe, in his *Westöstlicher Diwan*. Thus Marx's radical materialism is subsumed by a conception of the Orient that is Romantic or even messianic. In this view, Britain is fulfilling a grand mission in India, even when it does not know it is doing so, and India matters more in that regard than in the humanity or suffering of its people. India matters, that is, not for itself, but only as the pretext and focus of a British project:

> England, it is true, in causing a social revolution in Hindustan was actuated only by the vilest interests, and was stupid in her manner of enforcing them. But that is not the question. The question is, can mankind fulfil its destiny without a fundamental revolution in the social state of Asia? If not, whatever may have been the crimes of England she was the unconscious tool of history in bringing about that revolution.[65]

Britain's actions in India may have been selfish and brutal, but 'that is not the question'. Britain is the unconscious tool of a process much larger than itself, and its actions carry through what Hegel called 'the cunning of history'. This is a view of history that apparently encompasses West and East but which sees agency or authority residing only in the West. Said's point is that in spite of the patent political differences between Marx and, say, Cromer, the views of both are subtended by the same structure of thought about the relationship between the West and the Orient.

Early in *Orientalism*, Said asks this question:

> Can one divide human reality, as indeed human reality seems to be genuinely divided, into clearly different cultures, histories, traditions, societies, even races, and survive the consequences humanly?[66]

Orientalism is a prolonged study of the ways in which humans have made just such divisions, in historiography, philology, literature, politics. Yet Said concludes the book by reminding us that there is a large body of scholarship and writing that is not as oblivious to human experience as he reckons Orientalism is. Intellectuals can always break the bonds of their professional identity, or can shake off the vocabulary of their discipline. Writers and thinkers and academics can and do reflect on their own practice, and in this way guard against corporate thinking or the repetition of received ideas.

The Question of Palestine (1979)

The Question of Palestine has been described, by Said himself as well as by some of his commentators, as part of a trilogy of books, of which *Orientalism* was the first and *Covering Islam* (1981) the last. To the extent that all three books concern themselves with representations of the Orient, Palestine, and Islam, this is an accurate description. But *The Question of Palestine* is much more than simply a narrowing of the focus of *Orientalism* down to reference to one smaller country, region, or historical issue. It remains the most substantial openly 'political' book that Said ever wrote, though, again, it is crucial to realise that Said argued throughout his career for the relationship of even the most recondite texts with wider social and political contexts and movements. Furthermore, if *Orientalism* has been criticised for concentrating on the discourse of the West about the Orient, then it is important to see that *The Question of Palestine* itself embodies a 'speaking back', a countermanding of Orientalist discourse. It exemplifies resistance to a discourse of domination. This is dramatised most clearly and potently in the brilliant second chapter of the book, 'Zionism from the Standpoint of its Victims'. This long essay seeks to offer an analysis of Zionism from an angle or position that for a long time was occluded in accounts of that historical movement.

Said's point is that Zionism is most usually described as a movement and a history that culminated in the successful foundation of the State of Israel in May 1948. This is an example of what historians call 'Whig history': an historical narrative that seeks to explain the past as an ineluctable movement towards the present dispensation. The problem with this form of historiography is that it tends to see this movement as having been inevitable, progressive, and as justifying or legitimating the present. In the pursuit of this justifying aim, it tends to stress similarities between past and present, and in stressing the inevitability of its narrative, it tends to locate causation there too.

The purpose of 'Zionism from the Standpoint of Its Victims' is precisely to answer back to such a narrative but also to critique it. The emphasis on narrative is one that Said would return to, in other writings on Palestine and Israel. It is useful also in that it reminds us once again of Said's theorisation of narrative in *Beginnings*: the interplay between authority and molestation. It is not too crude to suggest that Said is arguing that the Palestinians stand as a kind of molestation of the authorising Zionist narrative. This view could be applied to Said's own efforts, as well. How does he characterise this work?

Said starts by arguing for the *locatedness* of Zionism, as a system of ideas. Every idea or system of ideas exists somewhere, he says, and is therefore 'worldly', intermixed with its circumstances, both historical and geographical.[67] Yet 'self-serving idealism' – *idealism* being the philosophical doctrine that reality is of the nature of thought – insists that ideas are never muddied or coarsened by reality. Said argues that this thinking is most attractive to people for whom a particular idea attains perfection, untainted by will or desire:

> Thus it is frequently argued that such an idea as Zionism, for all its political tribulations and the struggles on its behalf, is at bottom an *unchanging* idea that expresses the yearning for Jewish political and religious self-determination – for Jewish national selfhood – to be exercised on the promised land. Because Zionism seems to have culminated in the creation of the state of Israel, it is also argued that the historical realization of the idea confirms its unchanging essence, and, no less important, the means used for its realization.[68]

Said, in giving this account of Zionism, is describing here precisely the Whig attitude to history mentioned above. But, as he says, this kind of description of Zionism says very little about what the idea of Zionism, or the historical realisation of the idea, has entailed for non-Jews. Yet, '[T]o the Palestinian, for whom Zionism was somebody else's idea imported into Palestine and for which in a very concrete way he or she was made to suffer', this is the crucial matter.[69]

Said's approach is to suggest that powerful political ideas such as Zionism should be investigated in two ways. Firstly, '*genealogically* in order that their provenance, their kinship and descent, their affiliation both with other ideas and with political institutions may be demonstrated'. Secondly, 'as practical systems for *accumulation* (of power, land, ideological legitimacy) and *displacement* (of people, other ideas, prior legitimacy)'.[70] As was the case in *Orientalism*, Said here puts ideas developed originally in *Beginnings* to work in a more openly socio-historical context. Zionism, after all, has not merely been a practical political movement and effort; it is also a massive network of texts. What is necessary, he is saying, is a study of Zionism and its *authority*. Out of what history, circumstances, and network of relationships did Zionism emerge? By what means has it constructed its authority or legitimacy? What other or previous authority did it contest or displace? What are the factors that may molest that authority yet?

One of the primary difficulties in arriving at a proper critique of Zionism, especially for a figure of the intellectual Left like Said, is the way that it has become an article of faith for Western liberals – precisely the constituency that oppressed Palestinians would wish to address. It has attained this unique position because it has successfully occluded or made disappear 'the literal historical ground of its growth', its political, economic, cultural, and existential costs for Palestinians, and the militant distinctions it makes between Jews and non-Jews.[71]

The other great difficulty that must be confronted is the issue of anti-Semitism, and the relationship of Palestinian nationalism to the other Arab states. About the latter, Said is clear that pointing out the sufferings of the Palestinian people does not mean identifying with or legitimating conservative or authoritarian Arab regimes. Yet the general interdiction in the West on alluding to the victims of the Jews, in the era of genocidal assaults on Jews, operates to make it easy for liberal intellectuals to criticise oppressive regimes such as those of Cuba or Burma, while ignoring Zionist discrimination against non-Jews in Israel. But for Said, the 'task of criticism, or, to put it another way, the role of the critical consciousness in such cases is to be able to make distinctions, to produce differences where at present there are none'.[72]

Simultaneously, the critical intellectual must acknowledge the power and appeal of Zionism as an idea for Jews, and the richness of Zionism's fractious and complex internal debates. Mere blanket dismissal would preclude a proper understanding of Zionism's effectiveness, its ability to become hegemonic among both Israeli and diaspora Jews, and among Israel's supporters and admirers in the West. Said points out that he personally inhabits, in an amphibious manner, both the culture of the West, as an almost exclusively

Western-educated person, and that of Palestine, as an exile. This enables him to understand and focus on the history of European anti-Semitism and the 'intertwined terror and exultation out of which Zionism has been nourished', while also drawing attention to Zionism's 'other aspects'.[73]

To illustrate the liberal view of Zionism and Palestine, Said chooses the great English nineteenth-century novelist George Eliot. In *Daniel Deronda* (1876), Eliot works out her 'general interest in idealism and spiritual yearning', but in the context of Zionism.[74] Said suggests that Eliot sees Zionism as one of various potential projects aiming to create a secular religious community. Such a community would replace organised religion, which was reckoned to be waning in its influence. In her masterpiece, *Middlemarch* (1872), Eliot's heroine, Dorothea Brooke, is portrayed as imbued initially with yearning for a spiritually and intellectually fulfilled married life. The novel witnesses her aspirations being gradually tamed and domesticated, so that by its end Dorothea contents herself with a relatively ordinary life. But in *Daniel Deronda*, Eliot discerns in the Zionist project what Said calls 'a genuinely hopeful socioreligious project in which individual energies can be merged and identified with a collective national vision, the whole emanating out of Judaism'.[75]

Said notes that most of the characters in the novel – both Jewish and English – are portrayed as 'homeless', or alienated. But the Jews have retained a powerful yearning for their 'original' home in Zion, as well as a strong sense of loss at being cut off from that home. In this way, they embody a criticism of Europeans with their abandonment of any communal belief. The hero of the novel, Daniel, gradually learns about and embraces his Jewish identity, and 'when he becomes the spiritual discipline of Mordecai Ezra Cohen, his Jewish destiny'.[76] At the end of the novel, Mordecai dies, but Daniel marries his sister, Mirah, and pledges himself to working out his mentor's projects in and for Palestine. Said is particularly interested in two elements of this story. Firstly, in spite of her interest in the development in the East of projects of human socio-spiritual enlightenment, Eliot never refers in any detail to the actual inhabitants of the East generally or Palestine specifically. 'They are irrelevant both to the Zionists in *Daniel Deronda*, and to the English characters.' Further, '[B]rightness, freedom, redemption – key matters for Eliot – are to be restricted to Europeans and the Jews, who are themselves European prototypes so far as colonizing the East is concerned'.[77]

Secondly, in Said's reading, Eliot was only one of a number of famous nineteenth-century liberals or radicals, such as John Stuart Mill and Karl Marx, who abandoned their liberal or radical tenets when it came to lands and peoples outside of the West. But even more, 'Eliot's account of Zionism in *Daniel Deronda* was intended as a sort of assenting Gentile response to prevalent Jewish-Zionist currents.' Therefore, for Said, the novel indicates the degree to which Zionism acquired authority by means of its relationship with Gentile European thought.[78] In particular, Gentile and Jewish Zionisms agreed that there were no inhabitants of Palestine, or, more specifically, none of any political significance: 'their status as sovereign and human inhabitants was systematically denied'.[79]

What Said therefore takes from reading a liberal European thinker such as George Eliot is a set of ideas about Palestine and Zionism; namely, that

> Zionism is to be carried out by the Jews with the assistance of major European powers; that Zionism will restore a 'lost fatherland', and in so doing mediate between the various civilizations; that present-day Palestine was in need of cultivation, civilization, reconstitution; that Zionism would finally bring enlightenment and progress where at present there was neither.[80]

Said's wider point is that Zionism conformed as well as it did with advanced European thought in the later nineteenth century because of the attitudes to overseas territories and peoples both tendencies shared.

European Zionism made its bid for Palestine in the context of the greatest phase of European territorial acquisition overseas in history. Said points out that Zionism never at this time described itself simply as a Jewish liberation movement, but rather as a Jewish movement for colonial settlement in the Orient. Following from this, and crucially:

> [T]o those Palestinian victims that Zionism displaced, it *cannot have meant anything by way of sufficient cause* that Jews were victims of European anti-Semitism and, given Israel's continued oppression of Palestinians, few Palestinians are able to see beyond their reality, namely, that once victims themselves, Occidental Jews in Israel have become oppressors (of Palestinians and Oriental Jews).[81]

This is the ethical core of Said's argument. The oppression and genocide of European Jews does not justify their oppression of Palestinian Arabs. Palestinian Arabs should not be made to pay part of the price of European crimes of anti-Semitism. Palestinian Arabs have experienced the arrival in Palestine of large numbers of European Jews not as liberation, but as displacement, oppression and, in 1948–9, ethnic cleansing.

Said moves on to reinforce his argument about the affiliation of Zionist thought with European imperialist thought at the end of the nineteenth century. He suggests that for Theodor Herzl, the intellectual father of Zionism, even as the Dreyfus Affair brought him to full consciousness of the horrors of anti-Semitism, at roughly the same time the idea of Jewish colonisation overseas occurred to him as the solution to anti-Semitism. Herzl considered territories other than Palestine (in Latin America and Africa). In his diaries, Herzl argued that the natives of Palestine would have to be expropriated, and 'both the expropriation and the removal of the poor must be carried out discreetly and circumspectly'. Furthermore, 'we must spirit the penniless population across the border by procuring employment for it in the transit countries, while denying it any employment in our own country'.[82]

Said's argument is very similar to that he would develop in *Culture and Imperialism*, fully thirteen years after *The Question of Palestine*. He suggests that Zionism can be genealogically understood only within the context of imperialism. The latter, he says, depends as much on ideas and attitudes as on political and military power.

> Gaining and holding an *imperium* means gaining and holding a domain, which includes a variety of operations, among them constituting an area, accumulating its inhabitants, having power over its ideas, people, and of course, its land, converting people, land, ideas to the purposes and for the use of a hegemonic imperial design; all this as a result of being able to treat reality appropriatively.[83]

Said is suggesting that there is little analytical virtue in separating theory and practice in the area of nineteenth-century imperialism: 'Laying claim to an idea and laying claim to a territory . . . were considered to be different sides to the same, essentially constitutive activity, which had the force, the prestige, and the authority of science.'[84] Said points out the parallel between modernising attitudes in science and those in imperialism: the result was that both focussed on the sovereign European will and its ability to 'change confusing or useless realities into an orderly, disciplined new set of classifications useful to Europe'.[85] This issued in the production of taxonomies of territories, languages, and peoples, hierarchies of which the European was always the summit and the centre. European countries were reckoned to have developed faster and further than others, because of 'natural advantages'. European languages were superior to Semitic or African languages. Non-white races were significant insofar as they became objects of Western study, expertise, and knowledge, or as they were put into service providing labour-power for Europeans, or as they were moved around so as to suit European purposes.

Said provides many examples of how European travellers to Palestine viewed it through these lenses, even while it was a territory of the Ottoman Empire, and well before Zionism emerged as a movement and discourse. Repeatedly, Europeans refer to the degraded culture and barbarism, the stupidity and deceitfulness of the Palestinian natives, and their inferiority not only to Europeans but also to the Jewish population of Palestine. He concludes that Zionism saw Palestine 'as the European imperialist did, as an empty territory paradoxically "filled" with ignoble even dispensable natives'.[86]

Reading the texts of important Zionist leaders and thinkers, notably Chaim Weizmann, Said detects a number of patterns. Firstly, he suggests that Weizmann and others always saw the Zionist project not simply as creating a new Jewish society in Palestine (there was a Jewish population in Palestine in the late nineteenth century, but it was very small), but as a regeneration, a repetition, a return, a renewal. The land itself was to be redeemed, by Jewish labour and care. To achieve this regeneration and repetition, of the land, and of the Jewish community by itself,

> it was necessary to visualize and then to implement a scheme for creating a network of realities – a language, a grid of colonies, a series of organizations – for converting Palestine from its present state of 'neglect' into a Jewish state.

Furthermore, a particular sense of time, or temporality, was important to this project:

> The colonization of Palestine proceeded always as a fact of repetition: The Jews were not supplanting, destroying, breaking up a native society. That society was itself the oddity that had broken the pattern of a sixty-year Jewish sovereignty over Palestine which had lapsed for two millennia. In Jewish hearts, however, Israel had always been there. Zionism therefore reclaimed, redeemed, repeated, replanted, realized Palestine, and Jewish hegemony over it.[87]

So, Zionism has presented two faces. It has presented to the world its beneficence for Jews: it has provided an identity, a nationality, a culture, even a language, and a set of structures to make them possible. But to Palestinians, it has presented 'the other, dialectically opposite component . . . an equally firm and intelligent boundary between benefits for Jews, and none (later, punishment) for non-Jews in Palestine'.[88]

The result of this is that Zionism has been seen, by the Palestinians specifically but also in the Arab world more generally, as a purely negative phenomenon. What Said calls the 'internal solidity and cohesion of Israel' has been invisible to Arabs. Partly as a result of this, most of the Arab states have become quasi-totalitarian 'security states', where a multitude of inhuman and anti-democratic policies are justified in the rhetoric of guarding against 'the Zionist entity'. Equally, this bifurcation of Zionism has also had negative effects for Israel.

Institutions that pride themselves on their egalitarianism and humanism – the kibbutz, the Law of Return for Jews, the facilities for immigrants – are precisely exclusionary, discriminatory, and inhuman for the Palestinian Arab.

Said stresses that Zionism was and is not merely a general way of conceptualising Palestine as the home of the Jews. On the contrary, it is what he calls a 'discipline of detail'. To illustrate this, he refers to a document produced by Weizmann and other Zionist leaders in 1917, 'Outline of Program for the Jewish Resettlement of Palestine in Accordance with the Aspirations of the Zionist Movement'. Said discerns in this document the ambition not merely to colonise Palestine with Jews, but to *produce* a Jewish Palestine. He sees in the document a 'vision of a matrix of organizations whose functioning duplicates that of an army'. The document speaks of 'opening' the country to 'suitable' Jews. For Said, this recalls a Foucauldian disciplinary apparatus. It is an army, after all, that 'opens' territory and prepares it for settlement, that supports immigration, shipping, and supply, and, most important of all, that converts mere citizens to 'suitable' disciplined agents whose job it is to establish a presence on the land and to invest it with their structures, organisations, and institutions. For Said,

> Just as an army assimilates ordinary citizens to its purposes – by dressing them in uniforms, by exercising them in tactics and maneuvers, by disciplining everyone to its purposes – so too did Zionism dress the Jewish colonists in the system of Jewish labour and Jewish land, whose uniform required that only Jews were acceptable. The power of the Zionist army did not reside in its leader, nor in the arms it collected for its conquests and defence, but rather in the functioning of a whole system, a series of positions taken and held, as Weizmann says, in agriculture, culture, commerce, and industry.[89]

Said is offering us here a powerful example of Zionism's ability to effect what he called in *Orientalism* 'a *distribution* of geopolitical awareness into aesthetic, scholarly, economic, sociological, historical, and philological texts'. Hence we can now understand Zionism in the way we understand the discourse of Orientalism: '[I]t *is*, rather than expresses, a certain *will* or *intention* to understand, in some cases to control, manipulate, even to incorporate, what is a manifestly different . . . world'.[90] For Said, this amounts to the marshalling of the civil society of the Yishuv – the Jewish community in Palestine – into the elaboration of essentially military directive ideas. This is a particularly dramatic example of the capacity of Zionism to accumulate authority, land, and people, and to displace other or prior authority, people, and territory.

Said continues by outlining the emergence and workings of various Jewish organs charged with the production of a Jewish Palestine, and a nascent Jewish state in Palestine. Chief among these was and is the Jewish National Fund, which was created in 1901 with the purpose of acquiring land in Palestine and holding it 'in trust' for 'the Jewish people'. This foreshadows the Law of Return, promulgated after the creation of the State of Israel in 1948, which guarantees citizenship of Israel to all Jews, everywhere. The point is that such thought and such institutions were and are *extraterritorial*: the state that was born in May 1948 was not the state of its citizens, but the state of the Jewish people. This instantly made the non-Jewish citizens of the state second-class persons, but it also conferred on the Zionist state extraterritorial powers. After the state was born, very large tracts of Arab-owned land (whose owners had fled during the fighting of 1947–9) were assimilated legally to the state, and those Arab owners were declared 'absentee landlords', ensuring that their lands could never be returned to them by the JNF. What this amounts to is a highly successful effort to Judaicise and de-Arabise land.

We cannot deal in detail here with the complex, violent, and controversial history of the birth of Israel and the flight of the Palestinian refugees in 1947–9. What is interesting for us is that Said focusses on the need felt by Zionist leaders such as Joseph Weitz, director of the Land Department of the JNF, for 'transfer' of Palestinians out of Palestine, in order for the Jewish state to be demographically, politically, and socially viable. Again, there is heated controversy among historians as to whether or not Zionist forces put a coherent and detailed blueprint for 'transfer' into action in 1947–9, but Said's point is that such thinking reveals how Zionism envisaged the land and its prior inhabitants. Those inhabitants were reckoned to be insignificant, to have a tenuous relationship to the land. Initially, during the phase of Jewish migration to Palestine before 1948, they were largely ignored. When approximately 780,000 Palestinians fled during the fighting of 1947–9, efforts were made to make sure they could never return, both legally and also practically – hundreds of Palestinian Arab villages were bulldozed after the war. In Said's words,

> Zionism came fully into its own by actively destroying as many Arab traces as it could. From a nonentity in theory to a nonentity in legal fact, the Palestinian Arab lived through the terrible modulation from one sorry condition to the other . . . First he was an inconsequential native; then he became an absent one; then inside Israel after 1948 he acquired the juridical status of a less real person than any individual person belonging to the 'Jewish people', whether that person was present in Israel or not.[91]

Said argues that Israeli governmental policies since 1948 – such as the efforts to 'Judaize' the Galilee – have continued the subjugation of Palestinians within

Israel – so-called 'Israeli Arabs'. In the divisions and differences between Palestinian 'Old' Nazareth and Jewish 'New' Nazareth, for example, the Zionist-instigated separation between Jew and non-Jew is worked out in geographical and demographic terms.

Said's overall point is that a vast array of Israeli policies have been directed towards 'a maximum future for Jews and a minimal one for non-Jews'.[92] He discerns a strong continuity in attitudes to the Palestinians between the projections of early Zionist leaders such as Weizmann and the approach of contemporary Israeli soldiers and bureaucrats: to each, the Palestinians are negligible. They can be ignored, or, where not ignored, manipulated by social and military engineering. Legally, nationally, their existence is either nugatory or nonexistent.

Zionism has been so overwhelming a movement and idea for Palestinians that to struggle against it is very difficult. In 1984, Said published a long review essay in the *London Review of Books*, under the title 'Permission to Narrate'.[93] This was a lengthy consideration of a number of books arising out of the Lebanon war and the camp massacres. Underpinning Said's reading and analysis, however, was the linkage of *narrative* and *authority*, which we recognise from *Beginnings*. The American philosopher of history Hayden White, Said points out, argues that 'narrative in general, from the folk tale to the novel, from annals to the fully realized "history", has to do with the topics of law, legality, legitimacy, or, more generally, authority'. White notes also that, conventionally, the proper subject of historical narrative has been, following Hegel, the state.[94] Said is interested in his essay to note the competition and intertwining of the Israeli and Palestinian narratives, and his point is that the Israeli narrative had successfully interdicted the Palestinian one at the point of his writing because the Israeli narrative was underpinned by the authority conferred by the possession of a state. Said argues that the target of the invasion of Lebanon was the 'coherent narrative direction towards self-determination' of the Palestinian people with their history, actuality, and aspirations.[95] Competing against the Zionist narrative of Jewish in-gathering and return and redemption there has been the Palestinian narrative of dispersion, fragmentation, alienation, struggle, and hoped-for return. The Palestinian narrative, Said says, 'has never been officially admitted to Israeli history, except as that of "non-Jews", whose inert presence in Palestine was a nuisance to be ignored or expelled'.[96] With the military destruction of the Palestine Liberation Organization in 1982, the narrative of the transformation of Palestinians from peasants to refugees to revolutionaries 'has . . . come to an abrupt stop, curling about itself violently'.[97]

A crucial issue here for Said is the discourse of 'terrorism', which is capable of both absorbing and de-legitimating a narrative such as that of the Palestinians:

> Terrorism signifies... in relation to 'us', the alien and gratuitously hostile force. It is destructive, systematic, and controlled. It is a web, a network, a conspiracy run from Moscow... it can be used retrospectively... or prospectively... to justify everything 'we' do, and de-legitimize as well as dehumanize everything 'they' do. The very indiscriminateness of terrorism, actual and described, its tautological and circular character, is anti-narrative. Sequence, the logic of cause and effect as between oppressors and victims, opposing pressures – all these vanish inside an enveloping cloud called 'terrorism'.[98]

The point here is that societies, nations, and oppressed groups need to achieve a kind of narrative coherence in order to obtain socio-political prominence and legitimacy. The most powerful mechanism yet devised for instituting or institutionalising this narrative is the state. Thus Zionism struggled to create a state in Palestine, and the Palestinians struggle to create a rival state-in-exile, or a state-in-waiting, or, under the severely compromised Oslo Process, a 'state-in-Jericho-first'. Further, the established states have the power to regulate narratives, this power at its most extreme being that of designating groups or ideas that fall outside of the coercive or representational capacity of the state as 'terrorist' in the manner Said describes. If there is a linkage between states and narrative, then an important weapon in the arsenal of a state is the capacity to block rival narratives. Decades after Said wrote 'Permission to Narrate', we can still say that Israel successfully blocks and disrupts the Palestinian narrative.

The World, the Text, and the Critic (1983)

The 1970s was a particularly active and fertile period for Said. In this time, he published three major books. But he also was publishing at the same time a number of essays, many of them related to or developing ideas discussed in those books, some of which were collected in the volume *The World, the Text, and the Critic*. Notably as a collection of essays, this book necessarily is able to address a wide variety of sometimes disparate topics – most importantly the conditions of possibility of criticism and its politics, but also writers of interest to Said, such as Swift, Conrad, Renan, and Schwab. As a collection of *essays*, its treatment of these topics does not aspire to be definitive or complete. This permits Said a combination of, on the one hand, openness or vulnerability, and, on the other, polemical vigour in his writing.

The introductory essay, which we have already cited a number of times, is entitled 'Secular Criticism'. This term, along with the title words of the second essay, 'The World, the Text, and the Critic', sets out Said's concerns. Said's interest is in what he calls 'critical consciousness', a term that, as we saw in Chapter Two, bears the traces of his early interest in phenomenology, but which he places in a much more materialist context than either Husserl or the Geneva School would have done. Critical consciousness rises above and beyond the rough typology of criticism Said sets out – literary appreciation, literary journalism, literary theory – which represents a 'clear division of labour' and a structure of specialisation. This structure is part of a wider social ensemble, where literature and the humanities, and criticism, are held to ennoble a given culture, while also being marginal to its main political concerns. The acceptance by humanists of this marginality is consecrated and redeemed by the suggestion of their 'professional expertise'. To Said, this situation is unacceptable: 'For the intellectual class, expertise has usually been a service rendered, and sold, to the central authority of society. This is the *trahison des clercs* of which Julien Benda spoke in the 1930s.'[99] *Orientalism* is, among other things, a fierce critique of what Said saw as the state-worship of American foreign-policy intellectuals in precisely this matter. But the situation of the critic is somewhat different: the expertise of critics is based upon 'noninterference in what Vico grandly calls "the world of nations" but which prosaically might just as well be called "the world"'.[100]

The rise of 'literary theory' in the American academy since the 1960s has not improved this situation; rather, for Said, theory may even have hastened the abstract professionalism of criticism. Paradoxically, the origins of theory in Europe were 'insurrectionary'. Thinkers as various as Ferdinand de Saussure, Georg Lukács, Georges Bataille, Claude Lévi-Strauss, Freud, Nietzsche, and Marx were all critical of the traditional university, 'the hegemony of determinism and positivism, the reification of ideological "bourgeois humanism", the rigid barriers between academic specialties'. And yet what has happened is that American literary theory has 'retreated into the labyrinth of "textuality"', as represented in the work of Jacques Derrida and Michel Foucault, who Said accuses of endorsing their own canonisation and domestication.[101] By 'textuality' Said means the poststructuralist concentration on texts and the indeterminacy and proliferation of their strategies and meanings, as against an interest in the reality to which texts may refer, or the ideology they may express, or their historical status, or their material or institutional weight and effect.

'Textuality has therefore become the exact antithesis and displacement of what might be called history', Said says. Even if one accepts that history itself is largely accessible to us only as it is mediated by texts, as argued by Hayden White and others, Said argues that criticism should attend to 'the events and the circumstances entailed by and expressed in' texts:

> My position is that texts are worldly, to some degree they are events, and, even when they appear to deny it, they are nevertheless a part of the social world, human life, and of course the historical moments in which they are located and interpreted.[102]

American criticism, Said says, has turned its back on such issues. He relates this to the moment of 'Reaganism', that rightward swing in American politics at the end of the 1970s and in the early 1980s. To Said, it is not coincidental that a critical ethos of non-interference and pure textuality should have emerged in parallel with neoliberal economic and political practices of shrinking the state, reducing labour rights, and making free markets the guiding star of all policy. The result of this conjuncture is the abandonment by criticism of its constituency – the citizens of democratic states – to the mercies of consumerist forces.

Against this consensus, Said wishes to argue the connectedness of texts to 'the existential actualities of human life'. For criticism to avoid the forces that structure society is for it to fail itself: 'The realities of power and authority – as well as the resistances offered by men, women and social movements to institutions, authorities, and orthodoxies – are the realities that make texts possible, that deliver them to their readers, that solicit the attention of critics.'[103]

We need to take a number of points from these ideas. For Benda in France in the 1920s, the 'betrayal of the intellectuals' lay in their commitment to nationalist and – in the Dreyfus Affair – anti-Semitic fervour. Said cleverly turns this notion on its head: for Said, the 'betrayal of the intellectuals' in the contemporary West lies in their attempt to claim objectivity, neutrality, under the guise of narrowly defined expertise. If critical humanism defines itself by its 'noninterference' in the world, Said advocates 'interference'. Critical theory, in its 'insurrectionary' origins, offered precisely such interference, but it has been tamed and emasculated in the American academy. This narrative of the domestication and corralling of theory that once claimed to be a form of revolutionary praxis is perhaps the single most important framework in *The World, the Text, and the Critic*. Against the reification or ossification of texts and readers and reading that Said detects in even – or now perhaps most of all – poststructuralist criticism, he advocates a criticism that is alive to the subsistence of literature amidst a dynamic field of forces. We should note Said's suggestion that the text is a kind of *event*, and also his sense that texts are part of the moments in which they are *interpreted*. Said is suggesting that texts are historical both at the moment of their production and at that of their reception. In other words, the idea of worldliness affects Said's own writings, too. Their status, too, is dynamic, contingent, and not rigid.

Elsewhere in 'Secular Criticism', Said develops the famous discussion of the relationship between criticism, culture, and exile we saw in Chapter Two. Said argues that Erich Auerbach's exile from Nazi Germany and alienation in Muslim Turkey is crucial to his production of a magisterial work of humanistic scholarship, which also stands itself as an act of cultural survival. Auerbach wrote: 'The most priceless and indispensable part of a philologist's heritage is still his own nation's culture and heritage. Only when he is first separated from this heritage, however, and then transcends it does it become truly effective.'[104] Said argues from this that *Mimesis* was 'a massive reaffirmation of the Western cultural tradition', but also and at the same time it was based on 'a critically important alienation from it'.[105]

Said's discussion moves on to look at the term *culture* in order properly to understand this idea of critical exile. He first defines it as 'an environment, process and hegemony in which individuals (in their private circumstances) and their works are embedded'. We should note here the way that Said sees culture as geographical ('environment') as well as dynamic (a 'process') and related to ideological power ('hegemony'). Accordingly, he is interested in the ideas of *being at home in*, or *belonging to*, a cultural place. Culture is something one can possess. But it also has a certain power: 'the power of culture by virtue of its elevated or superior position to authorize, to dominate, to legitimate, demote, interdict and validate'.[106] Culture is here related to *authority*, as we saw that idea developed earlier in *Beginnings*, but also it is an agency of differentiation, in its ability to both legitimate and demote. In these matters, Said sees culture as a powerful system:

> What is more important in culture is that it is a system of values *saturating* downward almost everything within its purview; yet, paradoxically, culture dominates from above without at the same time being available to everything and everyone it dominates.[107]

This is the formidable structure which Said discerns beneath the apparently beneficent model of culture famously offered by Matthew Arnold in *Culture and Anarchy* (1869). In Arnold's description of the work of 'men of culture' as the dissemination of 'the best that is known and thought', Said reads the elaboration of 'the assertively achieved and *won* hegemony of an identifiable set of ideas, which Arnold honorifically calls culture, over all other ideas in society'.[108]

This identification of culture with hegemony goes even further. Via Arnold, Said identifies a dominant culture with the state, 'insofar as culture is man's best self, and the State its realization in material reality'.[109] Thus the power of culture is effectively the power of the state. This interdependence of culture and the state means that 'to be for and in culture is to be in and for a State in a compellingly loyal way'.[110] Said then offers a formulation that links culture, the state, and geography in significant ways:

> With this assimilation of culture to the authority and exterior
> framework of the State go as well such things as assurance, confidence,
> the majority sense, the entire matrix of meanings we associate with
> 'home', belonging and community. Outside this range of meanings – for
> it is the outside that partially defines the inside in this case – stand
> anarchy, the culturally disenfranchised, those elements opposed to
> culture and State: the homeless, in short.[111]

So Said is describing culture here as a spatialised system, which defines itself partly by means of that which it rejects and extrudes, and he is suggesting that the borders of culture are related to the borders of the state.

Said illustrates this conception of culture as a system of power with the example of Thomas Macaulay's infamous 1835 'Minute on Indian Education'. Macaulay was an English Liberal politician, who served on the Supreme Council of India, and during that time drafted a document – the Minute – in which he advocated the education of a small elite of Indians in English culture, so as to exert hegemony over the Indian masses. For Macaulay, Indian culture and literature were almost worthless:

> It is . . . no exaggeration to say that all the historical information which
> has been collected in the Sanscrit language is less valuable than what
> may be found in the paltry abridgements used at preparatory schools in
> England.[112]

In Macaulay's policy document, a rhetoric of belonging is sutured to a rhetoric of administration. For Said, then, culture is a self-reinforcing and self-authorising field of force, not merely the location of what Arnold famously called 'sweetness and light'. It is a process and location of the continuous reproduction of hegemonic values, which valorise certain ideas and practices and denigrate others.

Said argues that criticism is best located 'between the dominant culture and the totalizing forms of critical systems'. By this he means that the 'critical consciousness' partakes in some degree of Benda's model of the intellectual as a figure who transcends local or national cultures, in the name of universal humane values. But Said is aware of the limited effectiveness of this position for criticism, and he also believes that critical consciousness should not be merely some ivory-tower abstraction, but must be involved 'in the world', in the day-to-day struggles and debates of a given society. The point for Said is that criticism can properly be criticism *only* when it is involved in society and politics, but that it locates itself in this matrix in a reflexive manner. Critical consciousness places itself at the heart of its culture, but it is not simply the unconscious bearer and transmitter of that culture, but an historical, social, and political agent within it:

> And because of that perspective, which introduces circumstance and distinction where there had only been conformity and belonging, there is distance, or what we might also call criticism. A knowledge of history, a recognition of the importance of social circumstance, an analytical capacity for making distinctions: these trouble the quasi-religious authority of being comfortably at home among one's people, supported by known powers and acceptable values, protected against the outside world.[113]

Said is concerned about the relationship of criticism and critical consciousness with two related socio-cultural processes he calls *filiation* and *affiliation*. By filiation, he means that relation which seems to be natural or given to a writer, or a fictional character, or a critic, by birth, by tradition, by nature, by inherited location. By affiliation, Said means that network of relationships which human beings *make* consciously and deliberately for themselves, often to replace or compensate for the loss of filiative relations in modern societies. This can apply to a social organisation, such as a revolutionary party, or a professional grouping, or to an intellectual system or methodology. Said uses these terms to discuss the fate of criticism. He suggests that conventional criticism has tended to be filiative in structure: it has tended to set up a series of conservative relations between literature, scholars, and students, whereby great works of literature are conceived as monuments to be revered and appreciated, where critics are the guardians of these works, who initiate students into the correct attitudes to such works. This works then as a self-reproducing mechanism, most obviously in the university. The promise of powerful critical systems and theories is to replace this reverential filiative attitude with a comprehensive affiliative structure of understanding and interpretation. However, the tendency is for such affiliative structures themselves to become as formidably authoritative as the older filiative apparatus. So affiliative arrangements offer the hope of moving away from the older filiative structure, but often only end up reproducing it, albeit in a new form.

Said's point is that the role of the critic may be either to work in 'organic complicity' with the filiative mechanism of traditional culture – he or she helps to transmit legitimacy from filiation to affiliation – or he or she works 'to recognize the difference between instinctual filiation and social affiliation, and to show how affiliation sometimes reproduces filiation, sometimes makes its own forms'.[114] To work in the former manner is to seek to reproduce a traditional, monumental, reverential, canonical literary culture. To work in the latter manner is to open that culture out to the web of dynamic social, political, and economic human relationships in which it takes place and in which it finds its force and beauty. The point is that the critic is located at that nodal point, 'between culture and system', between the dominating aspects of culture and the state, on the one hand, and of intellectual and interpretative systems, on the other. The burden of *The World, the Text, and the Critic* is concerned with these issues. Repeatedly, Said returns to these themes, discussing Swift, discussing American 'left' or 'radical' criticism, in his lengthy consideration of Derrida and Foucault, and in his discussion of 'traveling theory'.

Said is interested in Swift on two grounds. Firstly, he sees the Anglo-Irish polemicist, pamphleteer, politician, and poet as representing 'the critical consciousness in a raw form, a large-scale model of the dilemmas facing the contemporary critical consciousness that has tended to be too cloistered and too attracted to easy systematizing'.[115] Said is interested in the dearth – at his time of writing – of advanced contemporary criticism of Swift. He sees Swift and his work, in fact, as resistant to assimilation by the discourses of contemporary criticism, and this is no disadvantage; it is, rather, part of what attracts him to Swift: 'He stands so far outside the world of contemporary critical discourse as to serve as one of its best critics, methodologically unarmed though he may have been.'[116] In the vocabulary of *Beginnings*, Swift's work functions as molestation to the authority of modern criticism. He and his work cannot be easily absorbed by such literary-critical categories as 'the heroic author', 'the text', or 'writing'. In fact, according to Said, Swift's work 'is at once, occasional, powerful, and – from the point of view of systematic textual practice – incoherent'.[117] To read Swift is to encounter a series of events 'in all their messy force', textual events that cannot easily be monumentalised. Swift's social role Said characterises as that of the critic or intellectual involved with but never in possession of power. Said is fascinated by the occasional nature of Swift's writings, the fact that so much of his work was reactive, that it was deeply embroiled in its moment of production, that it can be understood as most itself when seen as engaged in a complex network of forces, issues, personalities, and happenings. Accordingly, Swift was, for Said, the most worldly of writers.

Said is particularly interested in discussing Swift not as an Augustan satirist, or as a Tory advocate, but as an *intellectual.* Said sees in Swift an exemplary critical performance, or series of performances. For Said, many of Swift's critics 'pay too much attention to his ideas, and not enough to the deployment and disposition of his energies, to his local performances'.[118] Swift's capital, his resources, were principally intellectual and rhetorical – not material or financial – and the question for Said is how Swift used that capital. In Antonio Gramsci's vocabulary of traditional and organic intellectuals, Swift was actually both. He was a traditional intellectual, in that he was a cleric, but he was an organic intellectual in his closeness to power and to the Tory government between 1711 and 1713, and then, conversely, and later in his career, in his function as an Irish patriot and defender of the Dublin poor. But Said is also interested in Swift's resistance to contemporary literary theory. Against the prevailing tendency of various models of recent theory, whether deconstruction or Marxism, to see a text's surface as in contradiction with its hidden or interior meaning, Said argues that Swift's 'writing brings to the surface all he has to say'. Furthermore, Swift's most powerful critical method is to inhabit that which he criticises. So, most famously, in *A Modest Proposal,* he produces the most excoriating critique of the reifying and life-denying rhetoric of economic rationality, by arguing that the Irish poor should raise and fatten their children to be eaten. And lastly, Swift 'is always aware – and troubles the reader with the awareness – that what he is doing above all is *writing* in a world of power'.[119] Swift is one of the most positive images of the critical consciousness that Said offers in *The World, the Text, and the Critic*:

> In its energy and its unparalleled verbal wit, its restlessness, its agitational and unacademic designs on its political and social context, Swift's writing supplies modern criticism with what it has sorely needed since Arnold covered critical writing with the mantle of cultural authority and reactionary political quietism.[120]

Elsewhere in the book, Said's accounts of criticism are chiefly pessimistic. In 'Roads Taken and Not Taken in Contemporary Criticism', Said offers a balance sheet on the effects of the assimilation of continental European theory in American criticism. He considers that the arrival of theory in the American literary academy has contributed to a pervasive *functionalism* in American criticism. By functionalism, Said means a concentration on 'what a text does, how it works, how it has been put together in order to do certain things, how the text is a wholly integrated and equilibrated system'.[121] There are benefits to this approach: it has made serious and technical discussion of texts possible; it has done away with merely rhetorical testimonials to the beauty or wonder of texts; it makes possible the development of delicate and sophisticated critical vocabularies for dealing with texts.

Yet there are also risks attendant on such a view. The most immediate problem is that of criticism lapsing into scientism, or considering itself a science, in the model of the social or even natural sciences. Functionalist criticism, in acquiring densely complex professional vocabularies, cuts itself off from a wider public of non-initiated readers. Worse, the exercise of the functionalist critical methodology becomes self-justifying: 'You experience the text making the critic work, and the critic in turn shows the text at work: the product of these interchanges is simply that they have taken place. Critical ingenuity is pretty much confined to transposing the work into an instance of the method.'[122] Functionalisms also tend not to look beyond the borders of a text in order to explain it. This has the desirable result of compelling the critic to consider the fineness of the text's linguistic richness, but it also then suggests that the text's workings are wholly internal, and that it exists in an autonomous idealised space of its own construction: 'the text becomes idealized, essentialized, instead of remaining as the special kind of cultural object it really is, with a causation, persistence, durability and social presence quite its own'.[123]

It is against this kind of freezing of the text into the ossified object of a technocratic and narrowly professionalised critical practice that Said's whole argument in *The World, the Text, and the Critic* moves. In 'Secular Criticism', as we have seen, and in the title essay 'The World, the Text, and the Critic', Said's wish is to argue for a criticism that treats texts as dynamically situated historical and social phenomena, and that can be understood in the same terms itself. The aim is always to revitalise criticism and remove it from the deadening institutionalising hand of academic professionalism, and thereby also to remove literary texts from the reifying and monumentalising tendencies produced by conventional criticism. We saw in Chapter Two that Said's essay 'Reflections on American "Left" Literary Criticism', and his account of 'Traveling Theory', show that criticism's vulnerability to degenerating into functionalism and professionalism is closely related to its inability or unwillingness to theorise its relationship to the central authority of modern societies – the state – and also to the way putatively radical theories mutate when they 'travel' from one critical, institutional, and socio-political context to another. The main example of travelling theory that Said examines is that of Lukács's theory of reification and totality, but his essay also concludes with a powerful critique of Foucault.

Given that this is accompanied by an extended discussion of Foucault (alongside Derrida) in another essay in the collection, 'Criticism Between Culture and System', and given also that Said's name has been associated with that of Foucault, I shall look briefly at it here.

Said, who gives a largely (though not wholly) positive account of Foucault in *Beginnings*, and who deploys the Foucauldian concept of discourse in *Orientalism*, now offers a strong critique of the French thinker. On the whole, he is more interested in and positive about Foucault's approach to texts than Derrida's. What interests him is that he considers that Derrida's analyses suggest that the real situation of texts 'is literally a textual element with no ground in actuality', but for Foucault 'the text is important because it inhabits an element of power (*pouvoir*) with a decisive claim on actuality, even though that power is invisible or implied'. Accordingly, Said reckons that 'Derrida's criticism moves us *into* the text, Foucault's *in* and *out*.'[124] Foucault strives to present the text stripped of its esoteric or mysterious elements, and rather to force the text to 'assume its affiliations with institutions, offices, agencies, classes, academies, corporations, groups, guilds, ideologically defined parties and professions'.[125] Foucault presents texts not as part of some wholly or even semi-autonomous realm of textuality, or ideas, or *belles-lettres*, but rather as 'part of the social processes of differentiation, exclusion, incorporation, and rule'.[126]

However, although Foucault's suggestion of a relationship between texts and power is part of what attracts him, Said is not satisfied with Foucault's account of power (which dates mostly from Foucault's later work, in *Discipline and Punish* and the first volume of *The History of Sexuality*): 'Yet despite the extraordinary worldliness of this work, Foucault takes a curiously passive and sterile view not so much of the uses of power, but of how and why power is gained, used and held onto.'[127] This is a difficulty which Said attributes to Foucault's differences with, and final scorn for, Marxism. No matter that Foucault argues that power is something fluid, without a centre, not attributable to the 'privilege' of a dominant class. This is to ignore the wider issues:

> [T]he notions of class struggle and class itself cannot therefore be
> reduced – along with the forcible taking of state power, economic
> dominations, imperialist war, dependency relationships, resistances to
> power – to the status of superannuated nineteenth-century conceptions
> of political economy. However else power may be a kind of indirect
> bureaucratic discipline and control, there are ascertainable changes
> stemming from who holds power and who dominates whom.[128]

Said respects Foucault's wish to avoid an understanding of power that sees it simply as coarse domination, but he points out that what is lost in the effort is the appreciation that, even in modern capitalist, liberal-democratic, bureaucratically administered societies, there persists 'the central dialectic of opposed forces'.[129]

Said argues that Foucault's 'flawed attitude to power' is a product of the French thinker's vision of historical change. Foucault's model of *epistemes*, or unconscious epistemological frameworks that underlie all intellectual activity in a given epoch, in his early books such as *The Order of Things*, is unable to explain how or why the abrupt change occurs between one episteme and the next. In the later work, Foucault again argues, but from a different angle, against liberal or Hegelian or Marxist ideas of history, which all see the historical process as a progressive unfolding development with a positive *telos* or goal. Having disposed of the self-governing human subject, as the product of a mere confluence of discourses, Foucault is unable and unwilling to envisage a situation where human agents move self-consciously and coherently to intervene in history.

Furthermore, Said is prescient in putting his finger directly on the striking Francocentrism, even ethnocentrism, of Foucault's work. The parallels, Said says, between Foucault's carceral system and Orientalism are 'striking', but they are lost on Foucault himself:

> he does not seem interested in the fact that history is not a homogenous French-speaking territory but a complex interaction between uneven economies, societies, and ideologies. Much of what he has studied in his work makes greatest sense not as an ethnocentric model of how power is exercised in modern society, but as part of a much larger picture involving, for example, the relationship between Europe and the rest of the world. He seems unaware of the extent to which the ideas of discourse and discipline are assertively European and how, along with the use of discipline to employ masses of detail (and human beings), discipline was used also to administer, study, and reconstruct – then subsequently to occupy, rule and exploit – almost the whole of the non-European world.[130]

This critique of Foucault is deeply significant. It appeared originally in 1978, the same year that Said published *Orientalism*, often held to be his most Foucauldian book. Therefore, even before the wholesale assimilation of Foucault's thought to the American literary academy, Said was already formulating a major critique of the French thinker. Furthermore, this critique is not only one of Foucault's historiography and his theory of power, but it attacks Foucault precisely on the basis of his ethnocentrism. For Said, in a strong sense, this ethnocentrism is regrettable, but perhaps not surprising after all, as he sees Foucault's thinking on power as an example of the degradation of 'traveling theory', and as a 'theoretical overtotalization'.[131]

By this term, Said is suggesting that Foucault's thought becomes problematic at the moment when it moves from its discrete analyses and objects to wider socio-political questions. Said sees Foucault's work as a kind of *functionalism* of the kind referred to earlier: an attempt to describe the workings of concepts and institutions of power from the inside, so to speak; to look at the ways that power is deployed, the effects it has, the way it circulates in a social system, to see its coherences and continuities, and the ways it constitutes its objects. The things that are left out in this approach are the contradictions within this system of power, how it changes or evolves, whose interests it serves, and its edges or boundaries, where it breaks down and fails. Said objects that no theory is *ever* complete, hermetic, a seamless and faultless conception of its object, and neither is any mode of power ever completely all-absorbing – were it to be so, it would leave no position from which it could be identified, named, and analysed. Foucault's later thought, which posits power not as based in political institutions such as the state, but as a network of fissiparous connections where power is everywhere but never concentrated, weakens itself precisely because it has offered so overwhelming a picture of the functioning of power as to make resistance to it almost inconceivable. Characteristically, Said puts this in geographical terms:

> In fact, Foucault's theory of power is a Spinozist conception, which has captivated not only Foucault himself but many of his readers . . . Foucault's theory has drawn a circle around itself, constituting a unique territory in which Foucault has imprisoned himself and others with him . . . we must not let Foucault get away with . . . letting us forget that history does not get made without work, intention, resistance, effort, or conflict, and that none of these things is silently absorbable into micronetworks of power.[132]

Said's question for Foucault, therefore, is this: how is it that Foucault can conceptualise power so brilliantly – surely itself an act of intellectual resistance – if it is omnipresent and omnicompetent? Said sees in Foucault's 'overtotalized' conception of power and resistance a version of the Orientalist conception of the Orient, comparable to Conrad's view of the imperial world in *Heart of Darkness*: as an overweening apparatus that can only think of its object as its own creation, that can only think of its object as yet further fodder to feed and justify its appetites, that can only see resistance as an inverse function of its own power.

So, for Said, criticism cannot afford to allow theory to become a totalising explanatory system. For this to happen is to risk, in Foucault's case, becoming 'the scribe of power': that is, it is to risk the over-identification of a theory with itself, with its own workings and instances, and to that extent, with that which it purports to critique. At this point, for Said, thought has ceased and criticism is dead. Criticism must always be alive to its own ironies and weaknesses, and aware of the resistances to it, of the points at which it breaks down and does not exhaust the possibilities of its object. The best way for it to accomplish this is for it to maintain a sense of its worldliness, of its own status as a dynamic consciousness, located both historically and geographically. Said argues that criticism should be 'sceptical, secular, reflectively open to its own failings'.[133] The critical consciousness is restless and mobile, constantly renewing itself. It is, even more, the means by which a culture comes into being: '[C]ritics create not only the values by which art is judged and understood, but they embody in writing those processes and actual conditions in the present by means of which art and writing bear significance'.[134] Finally, criticism is *oppositional*, and it is liberating:

> In its suspicion of totalizing concepts, in its discontent with reified objects, in its impatience with guilds, special interests, imperialized fiefdoms, and orthodox habits of mind, criticism is most itself . . . criticism must think of itself as life-enhancing and constitutively opposed to every form of tyranny, domination, and abuse; its social goals are noncoercive knowledge produced in the interests of human freedom.[135]

Culture and Imperialism (1993)

There is a strong argument to make that *Culture and Imperialism* is the most 'worldly' work of criticism Said produced. It was his last major book, completed and published in the shadow of his diagnosis in 1991 with chronic leukaemia. He produced a large amount of work after *Culture and Imperialism*, but this is mostly either political journalism, very short works such as *Freud and the Non-European* and *Humanism and Democratic Criticism*, or the necessarily fragmentary and incomplete work on 'late style' (of which the book on Freud is actually a part). Said worked on *Culture and Imperialism* through the 1980s, giving lecture series and publishing essays that would go on to form chapters of the book. It is the work of a critic who had striven to open criticism and the literary academy out to the 'world', and who now had won a constituency on a global scale, by recognising that the 'politics' of the academy is always in a loosely homologous relation with the politics of the world outside.

In *Orientalism*, Said suggests that a general essay on the relationship of culture and empire has yet to be written. *Culture and Imperialism* must be seen, in the first instance, as Said's offered answer to precisely that problem. Its geographical scope is much greater than that of the earlier book: rather than concentrating on the Islamic Middle East, Said deals with English and French literature of the nineteenth and twentieth centuries that handles the imperial experience in the Caribbean, in Ireland, in North and Central Africa, in India and Egypt, in Latin America and Australia. A criticism levelled at *Orientalism* is that, in offering a powerful description and analysis of British, French, and American discursive attempts to represent and hold down the Middle East, Said fails to discuss Middle Eastern resistance – at the level of both discourse and action – to those efforts. Accordingly, *Culture and Imperialism* offers a lengthy discussion of resistance culture.

The later book is also methodologically quite different. If *Orientalism* was most famous theoretically for its heterodox relationship with Foucault's work on discourses, Said's work in *Culture and Imperialism* appears largely to have left Foucault's influence behind. This is evident at a number of levels. First of all, we can see this change even in the book's title. 'Culture and imperialism' holds echoes of at least two great books of British humanist cultural criticism – Matthew Arnold's *Culture and Anarchy* (1869) and Raymond Williams's *Culture and Society 1750–1950* (1958) – for which Foucault would have had very little time. Arnold famously suggested that culture – 'the best that is known and thought' – could also function as a conduit of ideological control or leadership, in a Victorian Britain increasingly fractured by class conflict. Williams, the later but more radical writer, suggests that the British tradition of thinking about culture needs to be wrenched away from a conservative tradition, featuring figures such as Edmund Burke, Thomas Carlyle, and Arnold himself, and shown to be more egalitarian and liberating, and dealing with culture as a complete way of life. Said's own use of the term 'culture and imperialism' partakes of both views in a complex manner.

For Said, *culture* refers firstly to the arts and practices of representation, description, and communication that are relatively autonomous from the economic and political world, and that often take aesthetic form. But secondly, *culture* can also refer to a hierarchical, refining tendency, which results in a kind of self-definition and aggrandisement. Said is concerned that culture in this sense is seen to work as a badge of identity, especially of nationalist identity. The paradox of this conception of culture is that it conceives of art as timeless, or as of universal human value, while also seeing cultures in hierarchical relations, where one culture is more 'valuable' than another. Furthermore, such thinking about art and literature is incapable of resolving the frequent dichotomies between the aesthetic productions of great figures of the Western tradition, such as Carlyle or John Ruskin or Charles Dickens, and their articulated political views, where they frequently opined in illiberal terms about the necessity of imperial expansion and the incapacity of subject races for self-governance. Said's effort in *Culture and Imperialism* is to bring these elements together.

Another difference from Foucault lies with the overall goal of *Culture and Imperialism*. If part of the purpose of *Orientalism* was to show the shared origins of Romance philology and scholarly Orientalism and their relation to European imperialism in the Islamic Middle East, *Culture and Imperialism* works as an attempt redemptively to *expand* the Romantic humanist tradition, a very un-Foucauldian move. Moreover, Said's insistence on the relative autonomy of aesthetic works compounds this trend. His main theoretical recourse is to Williams, and also Gramsci, whose work underpins the markedly more materialist sense of culture and geography which Said deploys in the later book.

The first chapter of *Culture and Imperialism* covers a great deal of ground. Firstly, Said is struck by how discussions of empire in the metropolitan West so frequently degenerate into what he calls 'a rhetoric of blame'.[136] By this he means that in the conservative moment of the 1980s, under the Thatcher government in Britain and the Reagan administration in the United States, debate about the imperial past tended to turn on how the countries of the Third World had radically mishandled their independence, lapsing so frequently into dictatorship, anarchy, and war after the great European colonial empires were dismantled in the period between 1945 and 1975. What was missing from the debate was an idea of what he calls 'overlapping territories, intertwined histories': the sense that the imperial experience had been mutual between the imperial centre and its colonial margins, that it had actually brought the European powers into a *relationship* with the colonised world that had not ceased at the moment of decolonisation. Equally forgotten in the shrill debates to which Said refers was the sense that imperialism had brought enormous changes and suffering in the colonised territories: vast population movements, profound alterations of economy and politics, not to speak of exploitation, massacre, and genocide.

Said is interested not in the content of these debates, but in their *form*. He suggests that this form can be usefully illustrated by looking at the form of Conrad's great novella, *Heart of Darkness* (1899). This narrative is one that is told in the mode of a seafarer's tale, delivered by Conrad's famous narrator Marlow, to a group of colleagues on the foredeck of the *Nellie*, anchored on the Thames. An anonymous narrator reports Marlow's telling of his tale. Marlow reflects on the difficulty of communicating with one's fellow human beings: he notes that 'it is impossible to convey the life-sensation of any given epoch of one's existence – that which makes its truth, its meaning – its subtle and penetrating essence . . . We live as we dream, alone.'[137] Nevertheless, Marlow 'still manages to convey the enormous power of Kurtz's African experience through his own overmastering narrative of his voyage into the African interior towards Kurtz'. Though Marlow's story contains many apparently minor episodes or digressions, what remains is its relentless forward movement: 'Whatever is lost or elided or even simply made up in Marlow's immensely compelling recitation is compensated for in the narrative's sheer historical momentum.' Ultimately, Said argues, Marlow's story enacts the story of empire at the level of narrative form:

> Conrad wants us to see how Kurtz's great looting adventure, Marlow's journey up the river, and the narrative itself all share a common theme: Europeans performing acts of imperial mastery and will in (or about) Africa.[138]

But Conrad's irony (related to his exilic sense of outsiderhood) undercuts and unsettles this apparent mastery. Said notes that in spite of its power, Marlow's story is located and dramatised. Marlow is not an omniscient, all-knowing narrator. He and his story are placed in a very specific location and time. From this, the reader can conclude that there is a space and a history outside of that story, although Conrad cannot yet imagine these, and leaves them empty.

Said suggests that two visions of the postcolonial world can be derived from *Heart of Darkness*. The first, more conservative, view accords with the confident movement of Marlow's narrative. Western visions of the postcolonial world that assert Western superiority, leadership, and political and cultural primacy mimic the apparent sovereign capacity of Marlow's narrative to encompass and represent everything in its dominion. The second, more radical, view takes its cue from Conrad's sceptical *situating* of Marlow's seemingly world-conquering discourse, both in history and geography. This placing of the imperial narrative allows the reader to realise that there is history that takes place after it in time and beyond it in space. Imperial narrative therefore becomes contingent, and, to that extent, contestable:

> Conrad's self-consciously circular narrative forms draw attention to themselves as artificial constructions, encouraging us to sense the potential of a reality that seemed inaccessible to imperialism, just beyond its control, and that only well after Conrad's death in 1924 acquired a substantial presence.[139]

This vision, taken from *Heart of Darkness*, leads Said to suggest the analysis of empire in what he characteristically calls 'secular' terms: all human experience is not only subjective at a significant level, but also historical and secular; it is open to analysis and interpretation; and it is not limited by national or regional boundaries. Nor is it susceptible merely to totalising interpretative systems. Rather than such systems, we need modes of interpretation that are looser, but that are also, precisely, secular. Interpretation must understand itself to be situated, 'worldly', even as are the objects of its analysis.

Said takes his controlling metaphor for the approach he is advocating from music. To deal with what he calls 'discrepant experiences' – the British and the Indian experiences of the Raj, for example – he argues for *contrapuntal* criticism. Contrapuntal music is music with many interweaving lines and voices; accordingly, Said is arguing for an interpretative method that can 'think through and interpret together experiences that are discrepant, each with its particular agenda and pace of development, its own internal formations, its internal coherence and system of external relationships, all of them co-existing and interacting with others'.[140]

Said wishes to place this approach within, and as a modification of, the very grand tradition of Romance philology and comparative literature that I discussed in Chapter Two. Going back beyond the great figures of the twentieth century in this field – Leo Spitzer, Erich Auerbach, Ernst Robert Curtius, Karl Vossler – there are the figures of late eighteenth- and early nineteenth-century European historical, anthropological, and comparative linguistic scholarship – Giambattista Vico, Johann Gottfried Herder, and Friedrich and August Schlegel:

> [U]nderlying their work was the belief that mankind formed a
> marvellous, almost symphonic whole whose progress and formations,
> again as a whole, could be studied exclusively as a concerted and secular
> historical experience, not as an exemplification of the divine. Because
> 'man' has made history, there was a special hermeneutical way of
> studying history that differed in intent as well as method from the
> natural sciences.[141]

Said points out that this tradition of thinking about literature and culture arose and developed over the period 1745–1945, and that this trajectory strikingly parallels the rise and development of both nationalism and modern imperialism. Yet the great *philologen*, from Goethe to Curtius, saw their idea of literature and their approach to its analysis as *transcending* national boundaries. Even Goethe's idea of *Weltliteratur* – 'world literature' – was deeply Eurocentric: the idea of human universality offered by the Romantic comparative tradition was nevertheless seen in European terms. Said points out that Auerbach acknowledged the existence of 'other' literatures in an autumnal essay just after the Second World War, but Auerbach's reaction to the 'emergence' of these other cultures was somewhat nervous. When the war and the Holocaust devastated Europe, literally thousands of émigré scholars fled to the United States. These included great European critics such as René Wellek, Paul de Man, and Erich Auerbach and Leo Spitzer (who both arrived in the United States via exile in Turkey). This intellectual migration brought the European tradition of comparative literature to the United States, yet flensed it of its sense of crisis. Said's point is that the Romantic tradition, even when transplanted to the United States, is idealist, accumulative, and self-authorising, but it is predicated on a trend in academic physical geography directly related to empire. Geographers such as Halford Mackinder – the doyen of British geographers in Conrad's time – and George Chisholm argued for the 'natural' status of a 'world-empire' headed up by the European great powers. Europe, they argued, was possessed of 'historical advantages' that allowed it to override the 'natural advantages' of many of the imperial territories, and conquer them. Geographical 'facts', it seemed, licensed cultural authority and superiority.

Said suggests that the task of secular interpretation is to articulate these two trends of thinking in comparative literature and geography.

> We need to see that the contemporary global setting – overlapping territories, intertwined histories – was already prefigured and inscribed in the coincidences and convergences among geography, culture and history that were so important to the pioneers of comparative literature. Then we can grasp in a new and more dynamic way both the idealist historicism which fuelled the comparatist 'world literature' scheme and the concretely imperial world map of the same moment.[142]

Using Gramsci's essay 'On Some Aspects of the Southern Question', Said suggests that the cultural and intellectual apparatuses and institutions of the European empires need to be re-interpreted: precisely because European imperialism's self-image was incorporative and synthesising and dominating, 'it becomes possible now to reinterpret the Western cultural archive as if fractured geographically by the activated imperial divide'.[143] Said envisages this interpretation in musical terms:

> As we look back at the cultural archive, we begin to reread it not univocally but *contrapuntally*, with a simultaneous awareness both of the metropolitan history that is narrated and of those other histories against which (and together with which) the dominating discourse acts. In the counterpoint of Western classical music, various themes play off one another, with only a provisional privilege being given to any particular one; yet in the resulting polyphony there is concert and order, an organized interplay that derives from the themes, not from a rigorous melodic or formal principle outside the work.[144]

The most famous example of this kind of re-reading that Said offers in *Culture and Imperialism* is his chapter 'Jane Austen and Empire'. Ingeniously reading an imperial context back into the work of a writer seen as embodying the quintessence of English literary culture is a way for Said to force the issue of contrapuntal reading, to bring it to the forefront of his critical purpose immediately.

The Austen essay is prefaced by a chapter entitled 'Narrative and Social Space'. This is a rich general discussion of criticism of narrative fiction. Said notes the proliferation of imperial references in English fiction. Defoe's *Robinson Crusoe* is only the most obvious example: Charlotte Brontë's *Jane Eyre*, Charles Kingsley's *Westward Ho!*, Dickens's *Dombey and Son*, *Great Expectations*, and *David Copperfield*, William Thackeray's *Vanity Fair*, Benjamin Disraeli's *Tancred*, and George Eliot's *Daniel Deronda* are all major Victorian novels in which imperial contexts feature. By the end of the century, with writers such as Conrad and Rudyard Kipling and H. Rider Haggard, and then early twentieth-century writers such as George Orwell and E. M. Forster, the empire is a very frequent theme in British fiction.

Said argues that the empire functions as a codified but rarely visible presence in much nineteenth-century fiction, 'very much like the servants in grand households and in novels, whose work is taken for granted but scarcely ever more than named'. In such fiction, colonial regions and subjects are depended upon by metropolitan regions and persons, but never considered worthy of historical or cultural attention. In such texts, empire is associated with 'sustained possession, with far-flung and sometimes unknown spaces, with eccentric or unacceptable human beings, with fortune-enhancing or fantasized activities like emigration, money-making, and sexual adventure'.[145] Imperial territories are realms of possibility, where younger sons or disgraced relatives are sent to win their fortunes or redeem themselves, to form themselves and to have exotic experiences. 'Contrapuntal reading' entails looking at such texts and examining them both for the metropolitan history and experience they represent and include, and now, also, for the colonial history and experience they shut out or idealise, and the resistance to empire that such texts and the authority they represent have provoked.

Investigation of this kind leads Said to come to some very striking conclusions about the relationship of the novel genre, in particular, with imperialism. His examination of *Heart of Darkness*, where he discerns both the idea of the European capacity and right to accumulate territory, and a self-aggrandising, self-originating authority that disguises such gross intentions, leads him to argue that such thinking is inscribed in narrative fiction as Conrad inherited the form. There are convergences, Said asserts, between the 'patterns of

narrative authority constitutive of the novel' and 'a complex ideological configuration underlying the tendency to imperialism'.[146]

The novel is the quintessential bourgeois literary form. Its characters are
noteworthy for their restlessness and movement. Said points out how this
movement is both geographical and social. He notes how, even with early
novels that do not appear to touch on the world outside of Britain, there is
nevertheless a parallel or homology between the values embodied in the newly
emerging novel form and the expansion of empire:

> in both realms we find common values about contest, surmounting
> odds and obstacles, and patience in establishing authority through the
> art of connecting principle with profit over time . . . we need to have a
> critical sense of how the great spaces of *Clarissa* or *Tom Jones* are two
> things together: a domestic accompaniment to the imperial project for
> presence and control abroad, and a practical narrative about expanding
> and moving about in space that must be actively inhabited and enjoyed
> before its discipline or limits can be accepted.[147]

When Said argues that the great English novel of the nineteenth century was
a significant and influential cultural *institution*, he is suggesting that the novel
had become by mid-century the major art-form in society, with a particular
capacity for representing society, reproducing its values and ideas, and dis-
playing its forms of authority. The novel projected a 'knowable community',
in Raymond Williams's phrase now re-inflected by Said. Part of this sense of a
knowable community was the representation of that community's boundaries
and of its sense of geography.

Drawing on the work of the historian D. C. M. Platt, Said argues that a
'departmental view' or consensus regarding Britain's relationship to its overseas
territories developed in the nineteenth century, and was given continuity and
presence in the novel. Platt argues that this widely held set of attitudes was
fostered by a variety of civil institutions and activities, including education,
journalism, and family bonds.[148]

Four consequences flow from this set of attitudes. Firstly, the empire is a
significant but marginal presence in English fiction long before its overt treatment in writers such as Conrad and Kipling. Further, the narrative techniques
of the latter are not unrelated to those of their major contemporaries such as
Thomas Hardy and Henry James whose writing appears to have no bearing on
empire at all. Secondly, contrapuntal criticism must see the novelistic representation of empire as part of a very slowly unfolding and elaborating tendency
in English fiction. The English novel seen as an aesthetic institution gives an
extraordinary picture of the continuities of nineteenth-century British society,

including its imperial relationships, and that continuity is sustained no less for the marginality of references to it. Thirdly, domestic social and economic order is frequently seen as related to an English order overseas. Fourthly, in wishing to avoid sweeping reductionism and to permit literary texts considerable autonomy, Said suggests that 'the structure connecting novels to one another has no existence outside the novels themselves'.[149]

As was the case in *Beginnings*, Said's concern in this discussion of the novel and empire is *authority*. Novelists locate their work in, and derive its authority from, the empirical reality of society, or, for Said, a 'carefully surveyed territorial greater Britain'.[150] Fictional authority is constructed, firstly, out of authorial authority – the author who gives narrative form to the processes of society; secondly, out of the authority of the narrator, 'whose discourse anchors the narrative in recognizable, and hence existentially referential, circumstances'; thirdly, out of the authority of the community, most often represented by the family. But the power of the novel also comes from its appropriation of historical discourse: the novel historicises the past, and narrativises the society. In so doing, it also differentiates and valorises social space.[151]

Underlying this fictional space lies real political geography. Geography is perhaps the key issue in imperial culture for Said:

> Imperialism and the culture associated with it affirm both the primacy of geography and an ideology about the control of territory. The geographical sense makes projections – imaginative, cartographic, military, economic, historical, or in a general sense cultural. It also makes possible the construction of various kinds of knowledge, all of them in one way or another dependent on the perceived character and destiny of a particular geography.[152]

This, then, is the thinking that underlies Said's mode of analysis of Jane Austen's *Mansfield Park*. The chapter on Austen exemplifies what Said calls 'consolidated vision'. But the geographical sense is also exemplified in Said's essay on the great Irish poet W. B. Yeats, which is part of the third part of *Culture and Imperialism*, on 'Resistance and Opposition'.

Said's argument is that in a novel such as Austen's *Mansfield Park* (1814), one can discern a moral economy of space, or of geographical reference. *Mansfield Park* is, as Said says, the most explicit of Austen's novels in terms of its ideological affirmations. Yet its publication comes many decades before the age of high imperialism, which many historians date from the Berlin Conference (1884). Said builds on the brilliant reading of Austen's novels in Raymond Williams's masterpiece, *The Country and the City* (1973), where Williams suggests looking at the representation of the life of the English rural gentry both from the viewpoint dramatised in Austen's fiction, and also from that of a figure such as William Cobbett, a radical journalist of the early nineteenth century, whose *Rural Rides* (published in serial form from 1822) documented the accelerating changes taking place in the English countryside. Williams, in other words, offered a reading of Austen predicated on ideas about land, estates, and agricultural capitalism. Said seeks to expand the horizons of such reading. He points out that

> *Mansfield Park* is very precisely about a series of both small and large dislocations and relocations in space that occur before, at the end of the novel, Fanny Price, the niece, becomes the spiritual mistress of Mansfield Park. And that place itself is located by Austen at the centre of an arc of interests and concerns spanning the hemisphere, two major seas, and four continents.[153]

The novel tracks the gradual assumption by Fanny Price of a central role and authority in the lives and home of her more fortunate Bertram relatives. In this process, Fanny herself is somewhat passive, but a wide variety of negotiations of geophysical and social space are conducted around her. It is this process that allows Said ingeniously to read the Antigua plantations that sustain the Bertram family and lifestyle back into a central place in the narrative. Repeatedly, Said notes the importance of space in the novel: Fanny's early confusion as signified by her inability to assemble a map of Europe; Sir Thomas's movements between England and the Caribbean; the dubious transformation of social space in amateur playacting made possible by his absence; the morally questionable social mixings and interchanges permitted by a garden maze. When Sir Thomas returns from ordering his Antigua estates, he promptly does the same at Mansfield Park. In Said's words,

> Austen here synchronizes domestic with international authority, making it plain that the values associated with such higher things as ordination, law, and propriety must be grounded firmly in actual rule over and possession of territory. She sees clearly that to hold and rule Mansfield Park is to hold and rule an imperial estate in close, not to say inevitable association with it. What assures the domestic tranquillity and attractive harmony of one is the productivity and regulated discipline of the other.[154]

Fanny's visit to her poor family and chaotic home in Portsmouth makes her understand more properly the qualities of life at Mansfield. She finishes the novel effectively the possessor of the great house, but she has not simply inherited this splendid location or authority: as Said points out, she has worked for it. The movement, acquisition, and employment of authority by Fanny at home are a small-scale domestic accompaniment to the larger activities of Sir Thomas: 'The two movements depend on each other.'[155]

For Said, Austen is to be interpreted as obliquely suggesting that 'no matter how isolated and insulated the English place (e.g. Mansfield Park), it requires overseas sustenance'.[156] In this case, the sustenance is provided by sugar plantations that, at Austen's time of writing, were worked by slave labour. Said quotes J. S. Mill's *Principles of Political Economy* (1848), where Mill argues that Britain's colonies should not be regarded as countries, but merely as outlying estates where Britain chooses to produce certain commodities. This is precisely the attitude Said traces in *Mansfield Park*. But the novel also prefigures other representations of colonial enterprise in English fiction. Charles Gould's silver mine in Conrad's *Nostromo*, and the rubber plantations owned by the Wilcoxes in E. M. Forster's *Howards End*, are later versions of the Bertram estates. Furthermore, Antigua has a place in Austen's moral geography. The Bertrams and their way of life would not have been possible without the trades in sugar and slaves. Sir Thomas is an absentee plantation landlord, a representative of a colonial class whose power and prestige were in fact waning by the early nineteenth century. Inter-imperial rivalries between Britain and France in the Caribbean, slave uprisings in Santa Domingo and other islands, the rise of the cotton economy, and eventually the abolition of the slave trade itself, all contributed to the decline of the class of which Sir Thomas is a member. His infrequent visits to Antigua are an index of his declining fortunes.

Overall, then, Said wishes to suggest that such a reading of *Mansfield Park* is not a matter of condemning it or Austen, but it is also a way of avoiding a pre-emptively and purely formalist, ahistorical reading. Such contrapuntal reading is necessary,

> if we take seriously our intellectual and interpretative vocation to make connections, to deal with as much of the evidence as possible, fully and actually, to read what is there or not there, above all, to see complementarity and interdependence instead of isolated, venerated, or formalized experience that excludes and forbids the hybridizing intrusions of human history.[157]

Equally, Said's reading of William Butler Yeats (1865–1939) is comparably alienating and controversial. The Anglo-Irish poet is most frequently understood, especially outside Irish literary studies, as a great European modernist. But Said wishes to re-inflect readings of Yeats to see him as the 'great national poet who during a period of anti-imperialist resistance articulates the experiences, the aspirations and the restorative vision of a people suffering under the dominion of an offshore power'.[158] For Said, Ireland's colonial history allows him to locate Yeats in the realm of decolonising intellectual activity. Said's essay on Yeats was initially published as a pamphlet by the Field Day Theatre Company in 1988. Field Day, founded by the Irish playwright Brian Friel and the actor Stephen Rea, is one of a number of intellectual movements in the contemporary moment – another would be the South Asian Subaltern Studies project in radical historiography – which Said sees as contributing to ongoing intellectual decolonisation in various parts of the former colonial world.

Said's discussion of Yeats focusses particularly on two matters. The first of these is nationalism. If Said begins *Culture and Imperialism* by arguing that the great European overseas empires produced a world of 'overlapping territories and intertwined histories', then his discussion of anti-imperial resistance is organised on the same terms. Empire, Said is saying, effectively produced the globalised world we live in today. The whole world – the Atlantic West as much as Africa or Latin America or the Middle East, is 'postcolonial' for Said. Nationalism, in all its variety, is a powerful socio-political force, but it is also compromised by its taking place on discursive and geographical terrain already mapped and set out by imperialism. Nationalist struggles across the former colonial world have been marked by certain regular characteristics. They have most often been led by native elites, educated in the politics and culture of the metropolis, who have found that their further economic and political development is actually hindered by the colonial relationship. Nationalist struggles have been conducted in pursuit of state forms and apparatuses put in place by imperial powers, and in terms of juridical regimes set up by those powers. What tends to issue from this pattern is the production of new independent regimes that are inverse images of those that they replace. Said understands Yeats to participate in both the initial nationalist push for independence, and then in a critique of the dispensation that emerges after independence.

Said's thinking about nationalism is influenced by the Martiniquan psychiatrist and theorist of decolonisation, Frantz Fanon (1925–61). In *The Wretched of the Earth* (1963), Fanon suggests that under revolutionary conditions, a decolonising national culture undergoes three stages: assimilation, self-discovery, and revolution. Said suggests that in the early stage of anti-imperialism, the decolonising intellectual typically comes to an understanding of European or metropolitan culture *as* imperialism. The anti-imperialist imagination, he tells us, is typically concerned with geography. This matches the geographical inscriptions of empire Said illustrates with his readings of the novel we saw above. Said cites the work of Alfred Crosby and Neil Smith to show just how powerful and totalising is the '*morte main*' of imperialism. Crosby's book, *Ecological Imperialism*, shows how European expansion brought with it not only imperial administrators and colonial settlers, but also a biological transformation; as new methods of farming were introduced, the agricultural economy was changed to suit European markets, new livestock species were brought in, new land law was established, and even new diseases arrived with the Europeans. The overall point is that colonised territories were alienated from their native populations not merely at the level of political sovereignty, but at the most fundamental levels of the ecosystem itself.[159] Said compounds this understanding with the work of geographer Neil Smith. In *Uneven Development*, Smith shows how historical capitalism has produced an unevenly developed landscape that combines wealth and poverty, industrialism and urbanisation, alongside agricultural degradation:

> The culmination of this process is imperialism, which dominates, classifies, and universally commodifies all space under the aegis of the metropolitan centre. Its cultural analogue is late nineteenth-century commercial geography, whose perspectives . . . justified imperialism as the result of 'natural' fertility or infertility, available sea-lanes, permanently differentiated zones, territories, climates, and peoples.[160]

Over against this 'second nature', decolonising writers, including Yeats, produce work that offers a 'third nature', or an idea of landscape and territory unsullied by imperialism. Yeats's early poetry in collections such as *The Rose* (1893) is suffused with a mythical sense of Irish history and landscape, and Said argues that Yeats is trying to resolve on the level of myth problems that he could not yet handle at the level of reality. Thus, rather than treating of Irish history and politics, he offers in his poetry a pre-colonial, pre-modern, indeed pre-Christian image of Ireland, a place of fairies, mythic heroes, and dreamy, vague, but beautiful landscapes. But this strategy is not simply reactionary: Said admires and expands on Seamus Deane's reading of Yeats in his *Celtic Revivals* (1985), where the tension between Yeats's idealised Ireland and the historical reality is seen as productive and compelling. Deane suggests that to Yeats, Ireland's apparent 'backwardness', in relation to the imperial metropolis, is exactly what makes it the platform from which the most radical critique of modernity may be launched. For Said, Deane brilliantly illustrates Yeats's 'super-terrestrial idea of revolution', a recovery of Irish national history and landscape at the metaphysical level, in compensation for the damaged and politically riven colonial reality.[161]

Yeats's explicit politics in the 1930s tended towards the authoritarian, and his sympathy towards Fascism has been the topic of aggressive debate since Conor Cruise O'Brien published 'Passion and Cunning: An Essay on the Politics of W. B. Yeats' in 1965.[162] Said, however, suggests that a way to understand Yeats's politics is in terms of *nativism*. By this term, Said means an essentialised cultural nationalism, frequent in decolonising cultures, which suggests that a return to a pure or purged past is the best means of resistance to metropolitan culture. Examples would include the Senegalese poet and politician Leopold Senghor's idea of *negritude*, which raised African values to a metaphysical plane in the effort to combat European cultural arrogance, or the Rastafarian movement in Jamaica. Said sees a number of problems with nativism. It reverses, yet accepts, imperialism's hierarchical distinction between black and white, or the European and the colonial. It is, finally, a betrayal or compromise of revolutionary promise:

> To leave the historical world for the metaphysics of essences like negritude, Irishness, Islam or Catholicism is to abandon history for essentializations that have the power to turn human beings against each other... Such programmes are hardly what great resistance movements had imagined as their goals.[163]

Said wishes to suggest that Yeats's later poetry can be seen as moving beyond the dead-end of nativism. He calls this second phase of anti-imperalism *liberation*, and it corresponds to an extent to Fanon's revolutionary phase of cultural response to empire. In Yeats's prolonged hostility to Britain, and the ludic, anarchic spirit of his late poetry, Said sees the dramatisation of the 'transformation of social consciousness beyond national consciousness'. Yeats's poetry 'struggles to announce the contours of an imagined or ideal community'. Said notes the instability of the sense of time in various kinds of revolutionary and resistance writings: thus, Yeats's extraordinary late theories of mythical time and millennial cycles in *A Vision* become in this perspective less eccentric and exceptional. Said's reading of Yeats is deeply informed by the ideas of Fanon, and though he sees Fanon as a writer more explicitly concerned with liberation, nevertheless Yeats also, even when he does not attain that liberatory moment of transcending his national condition, often prefigures it in his poetry.

Accordingly, Said is interested in the representation of violence in 'Leda and the Swan': violence as the necessary concomitant of change or the birth of the state, violence as the necessary engine of resistance. The question Yeats asks in 'Leda and the Swan' – 'Did she put on his knowledge with his power/Before the indifferent beak could let her drop?' – fascinates Said: how does the oppressed person or community learn from or repeat the oppressive force or power? But Yeats's poetry also 'joins his people to its history'. Yeats self-consciously offers his own life and experiences as symbolic of his nation's sufferings, reversals, and triumphs. Said quotes Fanon appropriately here: in the colonial situation, the claims of the native intellectual are not a luxury but a necessity in any coherent programme. The native intellectual who takes up arms to defend his nation's legitimacy, who is willing to strip himself naked to study the history of his body, is obliged to dissect the heart of his people.[164]

It is Yeats's accomplishment in this task that allows Said to argue that his work represents 'a major international achievement in cultural decolonization'.[165] As with Said's wish to force the issue of the geographical inscriptions of empire in Austen's *Mansfield Park*, a novel in which empire seems a marginal issue and presence, so too it is with his reading of Yeats. Said's effort is to wrench Yeats, a poet with a highly ramified presence in the conventional Anglophone literary canon, and relocate him on unfamiliar discursive terrain. Yet, contrapuntal reading notes also that Yeats was an English-speaking Irish poet, to whom the English literary tradition was of fundamental importance. To that extent, Yeats's poetry and his trajectory bear out Said's broader point about resistance culture: that it is frequently elaborated on terrain shared by coloniser and colonised. Mere nativism, predicated on a notion of complete separation between the newly independent society and culture, and the metropolis, is a dead end for Said. Total separation of cultures is a nativist fantasy: Yeats's national poetry is potent precisely because it works Irish themes, ideas, history, and mythology through a relationship with English (and European) poetic forms. Equally, Yeats's nationalism never prevented him from criticising his own society. At the level of *theorising* revolutionary resistance, Fanon's work is a powerful and unsettling mix of ideas taken from Marxism, Sartrean existentialism, and Freudianism, but deployed back across the divide against Europe. Said's attitude to postcolonial nationalism is directly influenced by Fanon's strictures in *The Wretched of the Earth* on 'the pitfalls of national consciousness'. Fanon argues that the decolonising intellectual must contribute not only to the formulation of national identity, but also must push beyond it, to the creation of a social consciousness at the point of liberation. Said agrees with Fanon that without this move, there is the risk that a once-revolutionary national consciousness may become a reified and dogmatic, state-centred and authoritarian 'pathology of power': decolonisation is debased to the replacement of one form of domination by another.[166]

In their different ways, modes of work, and locations, Yeats and Fanon – and other intellectuals of resistance that Said writes about, such as the Trinidadian activist and writer C. L. R. James and the Arab historian George Antonius – take ideas and themes, and also concepts and philosophies from the metropolitan West, and with them 'talk back' to the former imperial powers. This process, which Said termed 'the voyage in', is one which Said himself exemplified. He was fond of quoting Aimé Césaire (1913–2008), the Martinican poet, politician, and intellectual, who, in his *Cahiers d'un retour au pays natal* (1939), wrote that 'no race has a monopoly on beauty, on intelligence, on strength, and there is a place for all at the rendezvous of victory'. *Culture and Imperialism* is therefore a book which seeks to map the shared terrains of imperial and postcolonial historical experience, to preserve the complex and multiple characteristics of those terrains, while also suggesting modes of reading and understanding which offer 'freedom from domination in the future'. Said's most impassioned book is in this sense what the critic Paul Bové calls an essay in 'hope and reconciliation'.[167]

Chapter 4

Reception

The reception of Edward Said's work has been extensive and varied enough to provide matter for a book-length study in itself. I cannot possibly deal with every response here, but we can examine crucial and representative reactions to his work, from notable constituencies he addressed or for which his work had implications.

It has been *Orientalism* which has drawn the greatest attention, from soon after its publication in 1978. As was suggested earlier, it has been *Orientalism* which has shaped understandings of Said's career, which frequently has been taken as his most definitive statement on the Middle East, on cultural theory, on the academy, on literature. Yet *Orientalism* was only Said's third book, and now that his career is complete it is useful and important to try to retain an historical sense of the overall trajectory of his writing life. However, we should also note that *Orientalism* brings together and dramatises many of the most important concerns in Said's work: the canon of high European literature and its links with imperialism; the meanings of humanism and historical interpretation; the production and accumulation of cultural authority; the degradation of knowledge through its relationships with power and institutions; and representations of the Middle East. To this extent, critiques of *Orientalism* also have ramifications for other parts of his *oeuvre*. Critiques of Said's work have emerged from those disciplines where his work is felt to have had an influence or where he deliberately intervened. But his work has also been criticised on grounds of method and theory, and it is these critiques that will occupy us most here.

Firstly, though, we need to deal with the response from the discipline of Orientalism itself, and from its *doyen*, Bernard Lewis, who was among the contemporary figures whose work was analysed and critiqued by Said. Lewis accuses Said and others like him of envisaging Orientalism as a 'deep and evil conspiracy'.[1] He prefaces his remarks with a lengthy preamble, seeking to demonstrate a lineage of anti-Orientalist commentary in which he claims Said's book lies. Distastefully, Lewis suggests that the root of such anti-Orientalism lies in Nazi-associated anti-Semitism, originating in Pakistan in the 1950s.

Lewis charges Said with polemical recklessness and scholarly inaccuracy, and with attributing malice to individual Orientalist scholars in an unjustified manner. Said's choice of texts is arbitrary, Lewis reckons, concentrating on marginal figures and obscure texts. To claim that most Orientalists were in the service of imperialism is 'absurdly inadequate'. Avoiding discussion of German Orientalism is only the most egregious example of Said bending the historical evidence to suit his polemical purposes. Lewis accuses Said of mistranslating quotations from Arabic and German, and of slighting Arabic scholarship.

Said wrote a substantial reply to Lewis, where he sought to demonstrate the ideological substratum which lay beneath Lewis's purportedly Olympian and objective review.[2] What should interest us here is less the content of Lewis's critique than its form. He sees Said as an interloper in a discipline about which he knows an insufficient amount. He believes that Said is involved in charging individual historical Orientalists with a desire for dominance of the Islamic Orient. Yet Lewis has little to say about Said's individual readings. In his portrayal of Said's work as describing Orientalism as a conspiracy, worked out by malign intellectuals, he shows no interest in Said's effort to configure Orientalism as a discourse. That is, the epistemological and theoretical aspects of Said's work are entirely neglected by Lewis. Where Said wishes to suggest that the defects of Orientalism result from its status as a *discourse* – a body of textual and other statements with protocols, structures, regularities, and continuities that transcend individual contributors – Lewis persists in 'defending' Orientalism from what he believes are Said's charges of imperialism, racism, stereotyping, authorial wickedness, or error.

However, *Orientalism*'s impact was not just on the professional academic field of that name. One of the earliest, most penetrating, but also most sympathetic critiques came from the American anthropologist James Clifford. Clifford opens his essay by sketching a narrative of earlier analyses and critiques of the relationship between power and Western modes of producing knowledge of the non-Western world. His narrative begins with Michel Leiris, a French ethnographer and Surrealist thinker, who campaigned against the French colonial presence in Algeria, and worked with figures such as Jean-Paul Sartre and Aimé Césaire. In 1950, Leiris published an essay, 'L'ethnographe devant le colonialisme', in *Les Temps Modernes*, which 'announced a new situation, one in which the "objects" of observation would begin to write back'. The gaze of Western anthropology 'would be met and scattered'.[3]

It is in this tradition that Clifford locates Said's *Orientalism*, but he also appreciates the book's complex self-positioning. *Orientalism* partakes of Third World 'writing back' to the West, yet it 'should not be seen in terms of a simple anti-imperialism but rather as a symptom of the uncertainties generated by the new global situation'.[4] By this, Clifford refers to the global political situation at the end of the 1970s, when dozens of former European colonies in Africa and Asia had attained independence, a process which had also been overlaid by the ideological and economic divisions of the Cold War between the Soviet Union and the United States and their respective allies and client states. Simultaneously, he is referring to the intellectual outriders of these processes, where Western philosophy and political theory, including 'radical' theories such as Marxism, were being challenged by critiques from the decolonising world, and also from new European and American feminist, black, and student movements in the wake of the 'events' of 1968. Said's *Orientalism* – and Said's thought more broadly – sits athwart these developments in complex ways.

Clifford detects in Said a fundamental ambivalence between his admiration of Foucault (and behind that, an admiration of Nietzsche) and a strong residual humanism. Stemming from this ambivalence are what Clifford sees as Said's conflicting positions on cultural representation and empirical reality:

> Frequently, he suggests that a text or tradition distorts, dominates, or ignores some real or authentic feature of the Orient. Elsewhere, however, he denies the existence of any 'real Orient' . . . Said's concept of a 'discourse' still vacillates between, on the one hand, the status of an ideological distortion of lives and cultures that are never concretized and, on the other, the condition of a persistent structure of signifiers that, like some extreme example of experimental writing, refers solely and endlessly to itself.[5]

Yet Said's work dramatises in crucial ways the problematic of representations of the Other: 'The key theoretical issue raised by *Orientalism* concerns the status of *all* forms of thought and representation for dealing with the alien. Can one ultimately escape procedures of dichotomizing, restructuring, and textualizing in the making of interpretive statements about foreign cultures and traditions?'[6] Clifford rightly sees that Said is not setting out to offer alternatives to Orientalism, but rather to attack it from a variety of positions. Though Said is occasionally sceptical of *all* representation, he more often criticises Orientalism on the basis of its failure to attain 'personal, authentic, sympathetic, humanistic knowledge'.[7]

Clifford notes that Said downplays Orientalist scholarship that is sympathetic to its object, as represented in the work of figures such as Sylvain Levy and Marcel Mauss, but that he does give generous tribute to Louis Massignon. However, this raises interesting questions regarding Said's approach. Said acknowledges Massignon's profound interest in mystical Islam, and his campaigning efforts on behalf of oppressed Orientals, but he still argues that Massignon's work is finally contained and restrained by the discourse of Orientalism to which he is contributing: he is unable to avoid partaking of 'a will to knowledge over the Orient and on its behalf'.[8] This conclusion shows Said in his Foucauldian mode. But, according to Clifford, Said then asserts that Massignon could transcend his situation, both existential – as a Frenchman – and discursive – as an Orientalist – to rise into 'a broader history and anthropology'. The human being Louis Massignon could attain a full humanism. For Clifford, this is highly problematic:

> But the privilege of standing above cultural particularism, of aspiring to the universalist power that speaks for humanity, for the universal experiences of love, work, death, and so on, is a privilege invented by a totalising Western liberalism. This benevolent comprehension of the visions produced by mere 'local anecdotal circumstances' is an authority that escapes Said's criticism.[9]

Clifford shrewdly grasps the complexities and paradoxes of Said's deployment of Foucauldian ideas in the service of his humanist, cosmopolitan project. On the one hand, Said lauds the grand humanism of early twentieth-century European philology. On the other hand, partly because of the Foucauldian influence, Said also envisages culture as a totalising discourse of domination. For Clifford, this means that Said's wish to describe his conception of critical consciousness as 'oppositional' and as 'situated and responsible' can never be properly grounded or justified. It also compromises Said's ability to analyse constellations of knowledge and power pressed into the service of oppositional or decolonising movements.

Clifford also notes certain discontinuities between Said's *Beginnings* and the later *Orientalism*. He sees the phenomenological interest in intentionality in *Beginnings*, and Said's effort to preserve this concept in the face of structuralist and poststructuralist theory, striking a balance between individualist or subjectivist ideas of creativity, and external frameworks such as discourse or ideology, in the idea of a writer's career, or his endlessly repeated self-making every time he begins to write. But the authors analysed in *Orientalism* are not accorded this kind of dynamic subjectivity: though Said does allow them individual psychological depth, they are still finally seen as instances of discourse. Clifford closely examines Said's brief critique of Marx's Orientalism. Firstly, he suggests that Said is inconsistent to criticise Marx for his use of generalising, artificial categories, such as 'Oriental', 'Asiatic', 'Semitic', and also 'race' and 'nation', while not critiquing Marx's use of such concepts as 'class' or 'history', both of which are equally artificial and general. Secondly, Clifford points out the shift in Said's argument from Marx's Orientalist *statements*, to the matter of Oriental *experience*. For Said, Marx's natural empathy for the oppressed is overtaken by reified linguistic forms. Human emotion is displaced by a concept. Said's appeal to experience and authenticity is very un-Foucauldian; as Clifford puts it, 'Said's descriptions of Orientalist discourse are frequently sidetracked by humanist fables of suppressed authenticity'.[10]

These critical points allowed, Clifford nevertheless sees *Orientalism* as a crucial book for the problems it raises. He suggests that Said's achievement is less to undermine the idea of a substantial 'Orient' than to problematise the 'Occident'. Though Said's illustrious French contemporaries such as Foucault and Derrida set their theories of discontinuity and deconstruction within and against a totalised concept of Europe, Said himself 'permits us to see the functioning of a more complex dialectic by means of which a modern culture continuously constitutes itself through its ideological constructs of the exotic'.[11] This dynamic model, combined with Said's refusal to appeal to an authentic Orient and his suspicion of totality, makes his critique of essentialism and identity particularly powerful.

Lastly, and again very shrewdly, Clifford compares Said and Conrad, noting that any residual faith in culture is basically an act of willed belief, in an age of immense cultural change:

> It is the virtue of *Orientalism* that it obliges its readers to confront such issues at once personally, theoretically and politically. For its author, as for Conrad, there can be no natural solutions. Palestine is perhaps the twentieth-century's Poland, a dismembered nation to be reinvented. Said, like the Polish-English writer whom he admires and frequently quotes, recognizes that personal and cultural identities are never given but must be negotiated.[12]

Said – an 'Oriental' who seeks to dissolve the category, a Palestinian nationalist unaffiliated either to Palestinian parties or culture, a critic of the Western intellectual tradition who deploys the analytical tools of that tradition – himself embodies and dramatises 'the predicament of culture'.

If Clifford points out Said's ambivalent position between philological humanism and Foucauldian anti-humanism, Paul A. Bové takes the side of Foucault. He rightly sees Said as a crucial inheritor of humanism, but taxes him with failing to rise fully to the challenge issued by the French thinker. Bové's analysis of Said turns particularly on the essay 'Traveling Theory', but he sees in this essay certain traits that are given more sustained expression in *Orientalism*. Bové is interested in offering a *rhetorical* reading of Said's critique of Foucault's theory of power; that is, he is concerned to show how Said's reading of Foucault works not merely at the level of analysis but also at that of performance:

> Said's text enacts the struggle to establish the political efficacy of one conception of intellectual discourse and practice in the *very process of* establishing criteria by which the efficacy and history of theories can be judged. In other words, while 'Traveling Theory' argues that the test of a critical theory is its efficacy, it enacts a *textual* or *rhetorical* battle against, in the case of Foucault, an empowered antagonistic representation of intellectual practice, one that perhaps invalidates the immensely attractive image Said generates.[13]

Bové's point is that Said's critique of Foucault is a form of position-taking and self-assertion by Said himself, regardless of its accuracy as a portrayal of Foucault's ideas. Bové is interested in Said, here, as a particularly clear dramatisation of 'the unavoidably agonistic nature of high intellectual production'.[14] Bové sees Foucault and Said, in considerable measure, as 'intellectuals at war'. Intellectual production is a matter of struggle, not only in the material world, but at the level of discourse. Said's efficacy, and one of the reasons *Orientalism* has been so bitterly attacked, lies in his ability to delegitimate a range of discourses and practices from which intellectuals have traditionally taken their identity, position, and status.

   Yet, for Bové, Said's success in this manoeuvre is acquired at the cost of a certain conservatism. When Said draws a negative comparison between Foucault, on the one hand, and Noam Chomsky, on the other, his critique focusses on the hermetic, all-encompassing aspect of Foucault's theory of power. This theory leads Foucault, in debate with Chomsky, to agree that the intellectual's task is to offer criticism of existing social and political authority, but to refuse to offer an image of a future, alternative, and better dispensation. Foucault claims that any image he could offer of a better future would inevitably be tainted by false consciousness in the present. This is unacceptable to Chomsky, and also to Said, whose work Bové describes as 'the paradigm of all defences of the leading intellectual imaged as a competitor for social power and authority':

> Said continually argues for the social responsibility of the intellectual and cautions against the dogmatic potential of all theorizing, yet, at the same time, his metaphors reveal that continual contest and violence are the actual nature of the intellectual 'openness' he counterpoints to theoretical 'closure'.[15]

But Foucault, an erudite, prominent, and institutionally powerful intellectual, argued that such intellectuals as himself (or, one might say, Said) are actually obstructive of revolutionary change. For Foucault, intellectuals tend to arrogate to themselves the task of imagining alternative social and political arrangements for society as a whole, but they do so within a network of discourses and institutions always already hemmed in by and even complicit with power. In this formulation, leading intellectuals are most to be doubted precisely at the moment that they offer leadership, ideas, and organisation to a revolutionary movement. Foucault, therefore, seeks to undermine the role of intellectuals as Said sees it.

So Bové's critique of Said is that his understanding of the links between knowledge and power, most formidably set out in *Orientalism* but present throughout his work, is critical but not critical enough. Said's work, for Bové, offers impressive analysis of the varying degrees of voluntary and involuntary complicity of Orientalists with imperialist power, but Foucault's work goes further in undermining the entire economy within which both Orientalist and Saidian 'oppositional' work is produced:

> Not to struggle against this regime and its affiliations is inevitably to reproduce and extend it and the misery it causes. To imagine alternatives within it without at the same time struggling against it – by, for example, calling into question the seemingly highest ideals we have and desire – is not critical at all. Critique is practiced only when the appropriation of truth is at stake, not simply morals or attitudes.[16]

A poststructuralist critique from another angle is offered by Robert Young, in his book *White Mythologies* (1990). Young's project is a critique of Western historicism, specifically in its Marxist forms. By historicism, Young means a 'universalizing narrative of the unfolding of a rational system of world history', and he suggests that this may be seen as 'simply a negative form of the history of European imperialism'.[17] In other words, Marxism in its conventional forms is to be charged with a fundamental Eurocentrism – related to Said's critique of Marx in Orientalism – where it sees history as inevitably unfolding in European terms, and according to which, therefore, any deviation from this narrative is evidence of backwardness or aberrance. Marxism, the critical discourse of Western capitalism *par excellence*, is nevertheless apparently complicit with the universalising tendencies of European imperialism.

Young concedes readily that this is a problem identified by Said himself. In 'Orientalism Reconsidered', an essay published in 1985, Said wrote:

> So far as Orientalism in particular and European knowledge of other societies in general have been concerned, historicism meant that one human history uniting humanity either culminated in or was observed from the vantage point of Europe, or the West ... What ... has never

> taken place is an epistemological critique at the most fundamental level
> of the connection between the development of a historicism which has
> expanded and developed enough to include antithetical attitudes such as
> ideologies of Western imperialism and critiques of imperialism on the
> one hand, and on the other, the actual practice of imperialism by which
> the accumulation of territories and population, the control of
> economies, and the incorporation and homogenisation of histories are
> maintained.[18]

Said's core point here is that what he, quoting Ernst Bloch, calls the non-synchronous experiences and history of the non-Western world should complicate European conceptions of history as a grand story, a metanarrative, of which Europe or the West is the subject. Young agrees with Said that this is a major problem, but he considers that Said fails to address it properly.

Young suggests that the first problem raised by *Orientalism* is this: if the discourse of Orientalism is so enveloping, so successful in its monopolisation of the linguistic codes used to represent the Orient, is any other knowledge possible? Indeed, one may ask if it is even desirable, as to produce an 'alternative knowledge' of the Orient would be to accept the Orientalist premise that the region has a homogeneous identity. However, for Young, Said ends up repeating precisely the crucial gestures of the Orientalism he castigates: even to offer an account of Orientalism may be to repeat the essentialising gesture of Orientalism and to create a representation that can never match its object.

It is on the matter of representation that Young makes his next move. He argues that Said's work is compromised by ambivalence as to whether Orientalism is simply a discourse principally about and referring to itself, or a discourse that has some kind of purchase on reality. If Orientalism is a self-perpetuating and self-authorising discourse, then how can Said seriously claim that it has also been part of the Western effort to conquer, govern, and produce knowledge about the Orient? Further, if Said denies that there is any 'Orient' which could correct the misrepresentations of Orientalism, how can he claim that Orientalism is inaccurate?[19] Young, like Clifford, notes Said's humanism, and its irreconcilability with the Foucauldian model. One of Said's routine criticisms of Orientalism is that it denies the humanity of Orientals, and that it produces a kind of inhumane knowledge. But Young argues that Said's standard of humanism is derived from figures such as Matthew Arnold or Erich Auerbach, whose conception of high culture was predicated on a separation from the non-European world.

Young is equally stringent in his assessment of Said's conception of intel-lectual practice. If Said argues that the critic achieves detachment by means of 'experience' and 'critical consciousness', Young suggests that consciousness is a category that has been the focus of much analytical scepticism during the twentieth century, and that experience is only attained and understood through the mesh of forms of knowledge already agreed to be ideological:

> Said's difficulty is that his ethical and theoretical values are all so deeply involved in the history of the culture that he criticises, that they undermine his claims for the possibility of the individual being in a position to choose, in an uncomplicated process of separation, to be both inside and outside his or her own culture.[20]

In a related way, Young takes issue with Said's conception of 'the world', 'the text', and 'the critic'. For Young, such a grand book title suggests that the text and the critic could in some manner wish to be separated from the world, a never-fulfilled desire. But further, Said's positioning of 'critical consciousness' midway between dominant culture and totalising critical systems implies, according to Young, that cultures can be utterly dominant and homogenising, and that 'the only possible conflict can arise from the intervention of the outsider critic, a romantic alienated being battling like Byron's Manfred against the totality of the universe'.[21] Such a conception assumes that a dominant culture has no internal variations, contradictions, multiplicities, or fractures.

Young traces these problems to Said's essay 'The Problem of Textuality: Two Exemplary Positions', originally published in 1978, and later collected in *The World, the Text, and the Critic*, and re-titled 'Criticism between Culture and System'. This essay, Young reminds us, sets up a discussion of Derrida and Foucault, and favours the latter.[22] But elsewhere – in 'Traveling Theory', for example – Said rejects what he sees as Foucault's tendency towards a totalising model of culture. Young's point is that Said has to reject Derrida in order to continue to reckon that such totalisation is still possible. Derrida's deconstructionism would suggest that no totalising model is ever fully effective or hermetically sealed, but Young suggests that Said wishes to retain the idea of the completely closed system in order to pitch the individual critic against it.

For Young, this matter of closure is fundamental to *Orientalism*. He argues that Said cannot permit the writers he castigates so formidably internal complexity or productive contradiction – not even Marx – and this means that he does not so much undo the dichotomy between Orient and Occident as deny it. However, as Said nears the present – and himself – he must produce a more complex portrayal of great recent figures in the Orientalist pantheon such as Louis Massignon and H. A. R. Gibb. They are accorded the status of 'individual genius', and thus are able to transcend, to a degree, the discursive circumstances of their writing. But Said is also led to ponder whether any representation can ever be faithful to its object, at which point Young wishes to ask if Said's own portrayal of Orientalism cannot therefore itself be dismissed as a misrepresentation. Furthermore, Young finds parallels in Said's portrayal of Gibb's self-positioning vis-à-vis his Islamic materials – what Said calls 'strategic location' – and Said's own position, though in inverse terms: 'The Orientalist's misrepresentation apparently can be transformed into the critic's political intervention which dislocates the system.'[23]

Lastly, Young faults Said for failing to see that Orientalism really hints at an internal dislocation within European culture: 'If Orientalism involves a science of inclusion and incorporation of the East by the West, then that inclusion produces its own disruption: the creation of the Orient, if it does not really represent the East, signifies the West's own dislocation from itself, something inside that is presented, narrativized, as being outside.'[24]

Paradoxically, it must be noted that one of the most striking elements of Young's analysis of Said is his failure even to mention Said's own critique of Foucault's ethnocentrism. This is significant, for it shows that even as Said was deploying Foucault's ideas in *Orientalism*, and was comparing Orientalism to Foucault's conception of carceral discourse, he also saw Foucault's work as itself circumscribed and local. To this extent, Said does, in fact, recognise Orientalism as a dislocation within the West.

If critics such as Bové and Young see Said as employing poststructuralist ideas but failing to carry them to their logical conclusion, then Aijaz Ahmad's critique comes from a very different angle. Young's *White Mythologies* places Said, along with the other major 'postcolonial theorists' Homi Bhabha and Gayatri Chakravorty Spivak, as part of a wider critique of Western historicism, particularly but not exclusively its Marxist variants. Ahmad, by contrast, is an Indian Marxist who produced in 1991 a bitter and severe critique of the entire field of 'postcolonial studies', and of Said in particular. Much of what he objects to (including, in passing, Robert Young's work) is precisely the rethinking of history involved in the work of Said and those following in his wake.

Like James Clifford, Ahmad sees Said's work as sitting on the cusp of the global retreat of the Marxist Left and the parallel disenchantment of the Third World liberation movements of the mid-1970s. It is in this framework that he assesses Said's apparent embrace of Foucault and his ambivalent relationship with Marx and Marxist thinkers: unlike the more nuanced Clifford, Ahmad sees poststructuralism and Nietzscheanism as simply offering putatively radical thinkers such as Said a way of escaping or circumventing the Marxist tradition.

Like Clifford and Young, Ahmad places Said's relationship with humanism, and with literary humanism specifically, at the front of his critique. However, it is also worth noting that even in Ahmad's title – '*Orientalism* and After: Ambivalence and Metropolitan Location in the Work of Edward Said' – there is reference to Said's actual place of work and residence, and this will appear in deeply problematic ways later in Ahmad's reading. Ahmad notes Said's admiration for the great figures of early twentieth-century Romance philology, and Erich Auerbach in particular. He suggests that, in fact, *Orientalism* should be understood as a reply to Auerbach's masterpiece, *Mimesis*:

> The particular texture of *Orientalism*, its emphasis on the canonical text, its privileging of literature and philology in the constitution of 'Orientalist' knowledge and indeed the human sciences generally, its will to portray a 'West' which has been the same from the dawn of history up to the present, and its will to traverse all the main languages of Europe – all this, and more, in *Orientalism* derives from the ambition to write a counter-history that could be posed against *Mimesis*.[25]

By ambivalence, Ahmad refers to what he sees as the enormous paradox of Said's extraordinary and comprehensive critique of the European humanist tradition articulated in the name of values – humanism, sympathy, tolerance, cultural understanding – derived precisely from the tradition of which he provides such an excoriating account. In Ahmad's words, 'humanism-as-ideality is invoked precisely at the time when humanism-as-history has been rejected'.[26]

These problems are compounded, for Ahmad, by Said's invocation of Foucault. Firstly, Ahmad notes Foucault's own long-time anti-Marxism, before going on to argue that Said's deployment of Foucault is itself inconsistent. Said's positing a single discourse capacious enough to contain Aeschylus and Henry Kissinger is a contravention of Foucault's model: as Ahmad says, Foucault's theorising never reaches back further than the sixteenth century. But Ahmad suggests that what is at stake here is Said's effort to reconcile Auerbachian literary history with Foucauldian discourse theory: Auerbach does posit, in *Mimesis*, the existence of a steadily unfolding unitary European tradition of realist writing passed from author to author, from Homer to the early twentieth century. In Ahmad's view, Said is using Foucault to critique Auerbach, while retaining, in fact, Auerbach's historical structure.[27]

This contradiction then issues, for Ahmad, in what he sees as Said's vacillation on the matter of *representation*. He finds Said writing in *Orientalism* that 'as this book has tried to show, Islam *has* been fundamentally misrepresented in the past', and then shortly afterwards writing that '[M]y whole point about this system is not that it is a *mis*representation of some Oriental essence'.[28] For Ahmad, the second point contradicts the first. In a characteristic manoeuvre, Ahmad is not prepared to permit Said the complexity of a position whereby he can say that Islam has been misrepresented, while also not defending a unitary or monolithic or essential vision of Islam. However, Ahmad presses the point much further, and suggests that Said's interest not only in Foucault but in Nietzsche is discernable here:

> what Said is actually doing is drawing closer to the Nietzschean idea that no true representation is possible because all human communications always distort the facts. What happens between these two sentences is that Said raises the key question: 'The real issue is whether there can be a true representation of anything' . . . Said . . . in the midst of writing a history of Orientalism, is affiliating himself with a new kind of history-writing, which was emerging more or less at this time, which goes far beyond the empirical historian's usual interrogation of and scepticism about the available evidence and the accepted modes of interpretation; and enters the Nietzschean world of questioning not merely positivist constructions but the very facticity of facts.[29]

Ahmad is seeking to align Said with a full-blooded poststructuralist scepticism and anti-realism, in a manner that actually cuts against the tenor of his earlier demonstration of contradictions between Said's Auerbachian humanism and his Foucauldian anti-humanism. Unfortunately, it quickly becomes plain that what is at issue here is as much political as philosophical. Ahmad compares poststructuralist anti-realism to earlier variations on the theme, in Romantic, late nineteenth-century, and Fascist thinking, and concludes that it 'is significant that these anti-humanisms have come to dominate so much American scholarship on the eve of the unprecedented imperialist consolidations of the present decade'.[30] *Orientalism* – 'the very book which is doubtless the most influential among radically inclined cultural theorists today' – is held to partake of this 'irrationalism'.[31]

Whether *Orientalism*'s importance and influence – very great as it may have been – was on this scale at Ahmad's time of writing, or at any other time, is unverifiable. Nevertheless Ahmad moves on to suggest that *Orientalism*'s totalising vision of Western power-knowledge 'panders to the most sentimental, the most extreme forms of Third-Worldist nationalism'.[32] Even worse, *Orientalism* was not a publishing event, in the first instance, in the 'Third World', but rather in the metropolitan West. There, its constituency has been significantly and interestingly bifurcated:

> Its global authority is in fact inseparable from the authority of those in the dominant sectors of the metropolitan intelligentsia who first bestowed upon it the status of a modern classic; while, perhaps paradoxically, its most passionate following in the metropolitan countries is within those sectors of the university intelligentsia which either originate in the ethnic minorities or affiliate themselves ideologically with the academic sections of those minorities.[33]

Here is the 'ambivalence' Ahmad finds so distasteful. He is suggesting that *Orientalism* was a crucial ideological wedge into the Western – and particularly American – academy for Asian immigrant intellectuals. 'What the upwardly mobile professionals in this new immigration needed', Ahmad avers, 'were narratives of oppression that would get them preferential treatment, reserved jobs, higher salaries . . . For such purposes, *Orientalism* was the perfect narrative'.[34] Thus, Ahmad is able to dismiss Said's work, and postcolonial theory more generally, as the self-promoting discourse of bourgeois Third World immigrant identity, which, while having sloughed off the vocabulary of class, has found a new radicalism in identity or ethnic politics dressed up in poststructuralist garb.

This is Ahmad's supposed *coup de grâce*. Oddly, for a Marxist and one who loudly protests his belief in historical fact, Ahmad adduces no historical evidence or sociological argument for these inflated claims about *Orientalism*'s audience and readership in America. Sheer polemical aggression, it would seem, has clouded Ahmad's capacity for argument. This is a pity, because there is much in the questions he raises that is of interest and importance: Said's conception of history, the relation of his ideas of culture to political economy and capitalism, the historical context – both intellectual and political – in which *Orientalism* was produced. Unfortunately, Ahmad's critique does little to advance clear or constructive thinking on any of these areas.

Unsurprisingly and importantly, Said's work and *Orientalism* specifically have been subjected to feminist critique. Unsurprisingly that is, because Said frequently points out how the image of the Oriental as produced by Orientalism – irrational, sensual, dreamy, incapable of self-governance, decadent, primitive, childlike, beseeching Western regulation and tutelage – is often very similar to patriarchal representations of women in Western culture. Therefore, feminist critics and scholars were always going to take an interest in Said's work. Their responses have been varied.

Feminist critics, in common with others, charge Said with producing an image of the Orient and the Occident as homogeneous blocs. Most notably, Lata Mani and Ruth Frankenberg argue that Said should take into account internal variations in Orient and Occident. Furthermore, they note his concentration on the Islamic Middle East, and suggest that this focus means that his account is finally essentialist and reductive. Said extrapolates a general argument about Orientalism from treatments of one region and religion. The suggestion also is that Said represents discursive power in *Orientalism* as monolithic, one-way, and without contradiction or differentiation.[35]

Reina Lewis and Joan Miller, with differing inflections, seek to break up this supposedly homogeneous Saidian Orient, and Miller also argues that Said takes no account of the role of women in imperialist and Orientalist activity.[36]

Lewis interestingly suggests, in terms derived from feminist film theory, that the Western female gaze on the Orient actually subverts traditional patriarchal Orientalist authority of the kind that Said analyses. She points out that Said only deals with one female writer – Gertrude Bell – and in his commentary on her work never tackles her gendered discursive location.[37]

Against these criticisms, it must again be stressed that *Orientalism* is not, and never claims to be, a book *about* the Orient. Said would refuse such a description on at least two counts: firstly, that the book is about Western *discourse* about the Islamic Orient; secondly, that to suggest that the book is about 'the Orient' is itself to essentialise or attribute a spurious unity to a complex and densely textured region.

It would have been impossible for Said to answer the full range of critiques and responses to his work. But in 'Orientalism Reconsidered' (used as a foil by Robert Young to set out his own project of questioning Western conceptions of history, as we saw above), Said examines the effect of *Orientalism*, and also sets out what he considers to be extensions or elaborations of the work he had initiated. He revisits some of the circumstances, both personal and political, that helped to shape *Orientalism*'s production. He points out that he never intended his book to be seen – as it was seen in some quarters – as a defence of Islam or the Arabs. Rather, such categories as 'the Arabs', or 'the Orient', must be understood as 'communities of interpretation', as terms caught up in the politics of interpretation.[38] As an Oriental writing out of the Western-imposed muteness of the Orient, Said affiliates his work to a lineage of thinkers and historians and activists from the Arab world, the Caribbean, and South Asia, 'all of whom had suffered the ravages of imperialism and colonialism, and who, in challenging the authority, provenance, and institutions of the science that represented them to Europe, were also understanding themselves as something more than what this science said they were'.[39]

Said does set up a wider argument about the function of the Orient in Western concepts of history: for Hegel and Marx, and then for Jacob Burkhardt, Nietzsche, and Oswald Spengler, the Orient functioned in their theories as a site of antiquity and as what had to be left behind, 'a fecund night out of which European rationality developed'.[40] That is, Said is suggesting that modern European historiography, and other human and social sciences also, were constituted precisely on the terrain of this split. His work, and that of other critics of Orientalism, either alludes to or embodies 'the very history that resisted its ideological as well as political encroachments'.[41]

Said is cutting in his critiques of veteran Orientalists such as Bernard Lewis and Daniel Pipes. He points out that Lewis defends the objectivity and scholarly purity of Orientalism, while also himself being a Zionist and Cold War ideologue. Said argues that Pipes lacks the erudition of Lewis, but that he is much more openly ideological, and his work has 'a highly expedient sense of its own political relevance to Reagan's America'.[42] Said also notes that his Palestinian background has had an unfortunate effect on the debate about his book. Rather than noting the similarities between anti-Semitism and Islamophobia, some of his critics have taken the opportunity to defend Zionism, support Israel, and attack Palestinian nationalism (which *Orientalism* is held to represent).

Said goes on to set out the critique of historicism and its relationship with Orientalism which we encountered earlier in our discussion of Robert Young. Said's argument is that *Orientalism*, and work coming after it and in part inspired by it, amounts to the 'fragmenting, dissociating, dislocating, and decentering' of 'the experiential terrain covered at present by universalizing historicism'. Said identifies the task at hand as follows:

> we must . . . think in both political and theoretical terms, locating the main problems in what Frankfurt theory identified as domination and division of labour. We must confront also the problem of the absence of a theoretical, utopian, and libertarian dimension in analysis. We cannot proceed unless we dissipate and redispose the material of historicism into radically different pursuits of knowledge, and we cannot do that until we are aware that no new projects of knowledge can be constituted unless they resist the dominance and professionalized particularism of historicist systems and reductive, pragmatic, or functionalist theories.[43]

Said now refers briefly to a wide array of work in the humanities and social sciences which he sees as fulfilling such goals. Sandra Gilbert's work on the gendering of imperialist culture, Abdul JanMohamed's work on black and white fictions of Africa, Hanna Batatu's work on the Arab state, Talal Asad's work in anthropology, the South Asian Subaltern historians, Noam Chomsky's political writings, Fredric Jameson's theory of narrative, the postcolonial theories of Gayatri Spivak and Homi Bhabha: these are just some of the works that Said lists. This is a very disparate collection of projects, but in all of them Said detects a number of impulses or tendencies. The work of these scholars is interventionist in their disciplines: it 'posits new objects of knowledge, new praxes of humanist activity, new theoretical models that upset . . . the prevailing paradigmatic norms'. Such widely separated projects share 'a plurality of audiences and constituencies'; they share 'a decentered consciousness, not less reflective and critical for being decentered, for the most part non- and in some cases anti-totalizing and anti-systematic'; they are 'consciously secular, marginal and oppositional'; and they are political insofar as they 'intend . . . the end of dominating, coercive systems of knowledge'.[44] To avoid the potential reification of such necessarily specialised knowledges, Said finally advocates the crossing of political and disciplinary boundaries, methodological and theoretical reflexivity in regard to the conditions under which such knowledge is produced, and an activist sense of intellectual struggle, at both local and strategic levels.[45]

Such criticism was exemplary to Said, and much of it is indebted to his own extraordinary trajectory as an intellectual at the end of the twentieth century: perpetually initiating new projects, crossing borders both disciplinary and political, re-conceptualising terrains, attending to the margins, refusing established and emergent powers and orthodoxies alike, mobilising his unique combination of European and American cultural capital, on the one hand, and his Palestinian exilic consciousness, on the other. Late in his career, Said argued that contemporary sociologies of intellectuals spent far too little time examining 'the image, the signature, the actual intervention and performance' of intellectuals.[46] What Said finally offers his readers, in each instance of his writing, and in the entire writing career taken together, is a brilliant and exemplary instance of the intellectual life well lived, in all its richness, complexity, and commitment.

Notes

1 Introduction, life, work

1 See www.guardian.co.uk/world/2003/sep/26/highereducation.obituaries.
2 See www.columbia.edu/cu/news/03/09/edwardSaid_2.html.
3 Alexander Cockburn, 'A Mighty and Passionate Heart', www.counterpunch.org/cockburn09252003.html.
4 See http://query.nytimes.com/gst/fullpage.html?res=9D06E5D6153DF935A1575 AC0A9659C8B63.
5 Justus Reid Weiner, '"My Beautiful Old House" and Other Fabrications by Edward Said', *Commentary*, 108:2 (September 1999), pp. 23–31.
6 Michael Wood, 'On Edward Said', *London Review of Books*, 25:20 (23 October 2003), pp. 3–6.
7 Marina Warner, 'A Life for Freedom', www.opendemocracy.net/node/1511.
8 On critical 'interference', see Said's essay 'Opponents, Audiences, Constituency and Community' in Hal Foster (ed.), *Postmodern Culture* (London: Pluto Press, 1985), pp. 135–59 (pp. 157–8).
9 For an overall conjugation of these matters, see Joe Cleary, 'Edward Said and the Cultural Intellectual at Century's End', *The Irish Review*, 32 (2004), pp. 1–22.
10 Edward W. Said, *Power, Politics, and Culture: Interviews with Edward W. Said*, ed. and intro. Gauri Viswanathan (New York: Pantheon, 2001), p. 14.
11 Edward W. Said, *Out of Place: A Memoir* (London: Granta, 1999), p. xi.
12 *Ibid.*, p. xiii.
13 Edward Said, 'Between Worlds', *London Review of Books*, 20:9 (7 May 1998), pp. 3–7.
14 *Ibid.*, p. 3.
15 *Ibid.*, p. 3.
16 Seamus Deane, 'Under Eastern and Western Eyes', *boundary 2*, 28:1 (Spring 2001), pp. 1–18.
17 Said, 'Between Worlds', p. 4.
18 *Ibid.*, p. 4.
19 Edward W. Said, 'Vico: Autodidact and Humanist', *The Centennial Review*, 11 (Summer 1967), pp. 336–52 (p. 340).
20 *Ibid.*, p. 339.

21 Tom Nairn, *Faces of Nationalism: Janus Revisited* (London: Verso, 1997), p. 168.
22 Said, *Out of Place*, p. 3.
23 *Ibid.*, p. 3.
24 *Ibid.*, p. 4.
25 *Ibid.*, p. 4.
26 *Ibid.*, p. 5.
27 *Ibid.*, p. 7.
28 *Ibid.*, pp. 10–11.
29 *Ibid.*, p. 12.
30 *Ibid.*, p. 12.
31 *Ibid.*, p. 12.
32 *Ibid.*, p. 13.
33 *Ibid.*, p. 18.
34 *Ibid.*, p. 19.

2 Influences

1 Edward W. Said, *Joseph Conrad and the Fiction of Autobiography* (Cambridge, MA: Harvard University Press, 1966), p. vii.
2 Said, *Joseph Conrad*, p. vii.
3 *Ibid.*, p. viii.
4 *Ibid.*, pp. viii–ix.
5 Joseph Conrad, *Heart of Darkness*, ed. Paul B. Armstrong (New York: W. W. Norton, 2006), pp. 7–8.
6 Abdirahman A. Hussein, *Edward Said: Criticism and Society* (London: Verso, 2002), p. 25.
7 See Said, 'A Standing Civil War' in his *Reflections on Exile and Other Essays* (Cambridge, MA: Harvard University Press, 2000), pp. 31–40.
8 Hussein, *Edward Said*, pp. 27–8.
9 *Ibid.*, p. 50.
10 Edward W. Said, *Beginnings: Intention and Method* (1975; New York: Columbia University Press, 1985), p. xv.
11 Edward W. Said, *The World, the Text, and the Critic* (1983; London: Faber and Faber, 1984), p. 2.
12 T. S. Eliot, *Critical Essays* (London: Faber and Faber, 1932), pp. 14–15; quoted in Edward W. Said, *Culture and Imperialism* (London: Chatto and Windus, 1993), p. 2.
13 Erich Auerbach, *Mimesis: The Representation of Reality in Western Literature*, trans. Willard R. Trask (Princeton, NJ: Princeton University Press, 1953).
14 *Ibid.*, p. 557.
15 Said, *The World, the Text, and the Critic*, p. 6.
16 Said, *Reflections on Exile*, pp. xi–xxxv.

17 Hugo of St Victor, *Didascalicon*, trans. Jerome Taylor (New York: Columbia University Press, 1961), p. 105; quoted in Auerbach, 'Philology and *Weltliteratur*', trans. M. and E. W. Said, *The Centennial Review*, 13 (Winter 1969), pp. 1–17 (p. 17).

18 Said, *Culture and Imperialism*, p. 407.

19 Said, 'Vico: Autodidact and Humanist', *The Centennial Review*, 11 (Summer 1967), p. 340.

20 *Ibid.*, p. 341.

21 *Ibid.*, p. 339.

22 *Ibid.*, p. 344.

23 *Ibid.*, p. 346.

24 Erich Auerbach, *Literary Language and its Public in Late Latin Antiquity and in the Middle Ages*, trans. Ralph Manheim (Princeton, NJ: Princeton University Press, 1965), p. 12; quoted in Said, 'Vico: Autodidact and Humanist', p. 347.

25 Said, 'Vico: Autodidact and Humanist', p. 348.

26 *Ibid.*, p. 348.

27 *Ibid.*, p. 349.

28 *Ibid.*, p. 350.

29 *Ibid.*, p. 351.

30 *Ibid.*, p. 352; the term *Geistesgeschichte* means 'spiritual history'.

31 Said, 'Secular Criticism' in *The World, the Text, and the Critic*, pp. 28–9.

32 Georg Lukács, *The Theory of the Novel: A Historico-philosophical Essay on the Forms of Great Epic Literature*, trans. Anna Bostock (Cambridge, MA: MIT Press, 1971) and *History and Class Consciousness: Studies in Marxist Dialectics*, trans. Rodney Livingstone (Cambridge, MA: MIT Press, 1971).

33 Lukács, *The Theory of the Novel*, p. 88.

34 *Ibid.*, p. 41.

35 Said, *Beginnings*, p. 11.

36 *Ibid.*, p. 41; the quotation is from Marx, *The Poverty of Philosophy* (New York: International Publishers, 1963), p. 109.

37 Said, 'Beginnings' in *Power, Politics and Culture: Interviews with Edward W. Said*, ed. and intro. Gauri Viswanathan (New York: Pantheon, 2001), pp. 3–38 (p. 17).

38 Said, *Orientalism* (1978; London: Penguin, 2003), p. 16.

39 Said, 'Traveling Theory' in *The World, the Text, and the Critic*, pp. 226–47 (p. 235).

40 *Ibid.*, p. 238.

41 *Ibid.*, pp. 238–9.

42 Said, 'Traveling Theory Reconsidered' in his *Reflections on Exile*, pp. 435–52; originally published in Robert Polhemus and Roger Henkle (eds.), *Critical Reconstructions: The Relationship of Fiction and Life* (Palo Alto, CA: Stanford University Press, 1994).

43 Said, 'Traveling Theory Reconsidered', p. 438.

44 *Ibid.*, p. 438.

45 *Ibid.*, pp. 440–1.

46 *Ibid.*, p. 442.

47 *Ibid.*, p. 444.
48 See Said, 'Adorno as Lateness Itself' in Nigel Gibson and Andrew Rubin (eds.), *Adorno: A Critical Reader* (Oxford: Blackwell, 2002), pp. 193–208; also Said, 'On Lost Causes' in his *Reflections on Exile*, pp. 527–53; also Said, *Freud and the Non-European* (London: Verso, 2003).
49 See Antonio Gramsci, *Selections from the Prison Notebooks*, ed. and trans. Quentin Hoare and Geoffrey Nowell Smith (London: Lawrence and Wishart, 1971).
50 Gramsci, *Selections*, p. 5.
51 Said, *Orientalism*, p. 7.
52 *Ibid.*, p. 11.
53 *Ibid.*, p. 11.
54 *Ibid.*, p. 12.
55 Said, 'Opponents, Audiences, Constituencies and Community' in his *Reflections on Exile*, pp. 118–47 (p. 129).
56 Said, 'Opponents, Audiences, Constituencies and Community', p. 130.
57 Said, 'Reflections on American "Left" Literary Criticism' in his *The World, the Text, and the Critic*, pp. 158–77 (p. 159).
58 Said, 'Reflections', p. 160.
59 *Ibid.*, p. 169.
60 *Ibid.*, p. 170.
61 *Ibid.*, p. 171.
62 *Ibid.*, p. 174.
63 *Ibid.*, p. 174.
64 *Ibid.*, p. 175.
65 *Ibid.*, p. 171.
66 Said, *Musical Elaborations* (London: Chatto and Windus, 1991).
67 *Ibid.*, p. xiii.
68 *Ibid.*, p. xiv.
69 *Ibid.*, p. xiv.
70 *Ibid.*, p. xv.
71 *Ibid.*, pp. 13–14.
72 *Ibid.*, p. 19.
73 *Ibid.*, pp. 20–1.
74 *Ibid.*, p. 27.
75 See Theodor Adorno, 'Late Style in Beethoven' in Richard Leppert (ed.), *Essays on Music* (Berkeley: University of California Press, 2002), pp. 564–8.
76 Edward W. Said, *On Late Style* (London: Bloomsbury, 2006).
77 Said, 'On Lost Causes' in his *Reflections on Exile*, pp. 527–53; Said, 'Adorno as Lateness Itself' in Nigel Gibson and Andrew Rubin (eds.), *Adorno: A Critical Reader* (Oxford: Blackwell, 2002), pp. 193–208; Said, *Freud and the Non-European* (London: Verso, 2003).
78 Said, 'Adorno as Lateness Itself', p. 196.
79 *Ibid.*, pp. 196–7.

80 *Ibid.*, p. 198.

81 Adorno, 'Late Style in Beethoven', p. 567.

82 Said, 'Adorno as Lateness Itself', p. 200.

83 *Ibid.*, p. 201.

84 Said, *Representations of the Intellectual: The 1993 Reith Lectures* (New York: Pantheon, 1994), pp. 55–7.

85 Said, 'Adorno as Lateness Itself', p. 204.

86 *Ibid.*, p. 206.

87 Adorno, 'Resignation' in his *Critical Models: Interventions and Catchwords* (New York: Columbia University Press, 1998), pp. 289–93 (p. 293).

88 Said, 'Adorno as Lateness Itself', pp. 206–7.

89 The West-Eastern Divan, an orchestra composed of young Israeli and Arab musicians and named after a novel by Johann Wolfgang von Goethe, arose out of a workshop directed by Said and Barenboim in Weimar in 1999.

90 Said, 'My Right of Return', interview with Ari Shavit, *Ha'aretz Magazine* (18 August 2000), p. 16; collected in Said, *Power, Politics, and Culture*, ed. Viswanathan, p. 458.

91 Said, *Beginnings*, p. 282.

92 *Ibid.*, p. 290.

93 *Ibid.*, p. 294.

94 *Ibid.*, p. 294.

95 *Ibid.*, p. 301.

96 *Ibid.*, p. 296.

97 *Ibid.*, pp. 296–7.

98 *Ibid.*, p. 293.

99 *Ibid.*, p. 291.

100 Michel Foucault, 'What is an Author?' in his *Language, Counter-Memory, Practice: Selected Essays and Interviews*, ed. Donald Bouchard (Ithaca, NY: Cornell University Press, 1977), pp. 113–38 (pp. 131–2).

101 Foucault, 'Nietzsche, Genealogy, History' in his *Language, Counter-Memory, Practice*, pp. 139–64 (p. 164); quoted in Said, *Beginnings*, p. 296.

102 See Foucault, 'The Order of Discourse' in Robert Young (ed.), *Untying the Text: A Poststructuralist Reader* (London: Routledge and Kegan Paul, 1981), pp. 48–78.

103 Said, *Beginnings*, p. 302.

104 *Ibid.*, pp. 308–9.

105 *Ibid.*, p. 291.

106 *Ibid.*, p. 295.

107 *Ibid.*, p. 310.

108 *Ibid.*, p. 292.

109 *Ibid.*, p. 288.

110 *Ibid.*, p. 308.

111 *Ibid.*, p. 283.

3 Works

1 Timothy Brennan, 'Places of Mind, Occupied Lands: Edward Said and Philology' in Michael Sprinker (ed.), *Edward Said: A Critical Reader* (Oxford: Blackwell, 1992), pp. 74–95 (p. 74).
2 See *Diacritics* 6:3 (Fall 1976).
3 Said, *Beginnings*, p. 5.
4 *Ibid.*, p. 6.
5 *Ibid.*, p. 12.
6 J. Hillis Miller, 'Beginning with a Text', collected in his *Theory Now and Then* (Durham, NC: Duke University Press, 1991), pp. 133–42 (p. 137).
7 Said, *Beginnings*, p. 17.
8 Miller, 'Beginning with a Text', p. 134.
9 Said, *Beginnings*, p. 22.
10 *Ibid.*, p. 23.
11 *Ibid.*, p. 23.
12 *Ibid.*, p. 24.
13 *Ibid.*, p. 24.
14 *Ibid.*, p. 25.
15 *Ibid.*, p. 82.
16 *Ibid.*, p. 83.
17 *Ibid.*, pp. 88–9.
18 *Ibid.*, pp. 92–3.
19 *Ibid.*, p. 93.
20 *Ibid.*, p. 94.
21 *Ibid.*, p. 94.
22 *Ibid.*, pp. 94–5.
23 *Ibid.*, p. 98.
24 *Ibid.*, p. 98.
25 *Ibid.*, p. 99.
26 *Ibid.*, pp. 99–100.
27 *Ibid.*, p. 100.
28 *Ibid.*, p. 152.
29 *Ibid.*, p. 24.
30 Said, *Orientalism*, p. 330.
31 *Ibid.*, pp. 2–3.
32 *Ibid.*, p. 4.
33 *Ibid.*, p. 5.
34 *Ibid.*, p. 6.
35 *Ibid.*, p. 3.
36 *Ibid.*, p. 3.
37 *Ibid.*, p. 12.
38 *Ibid.*, p. 15.

39 *Ibid.*, p. 16.
40 *Ibid.*, p. 18.
41 *Ibid.*, pp. 19–20.
42 *Ibid.*, p. 20.
43 *Ibid.*, p. 20.
44 *Ibid.*, p. 22.
45 *Ibid.*, p. 23.
46 Antonio Gramsci, *Selections from the Prison Notebooks*, trans. and ed. Quentin Hoare and Geoffrey Nowell Smith (London: Lawrence and Wishart, 1971), p. 324; quoted in Said, *Orientalism*, p. 25.
47 Said, *Orientalism*, p. 80.
48 *Ibid.*, p. 86.
49 *Ibid.*, p. 88.
50 *Ibid.*, p. 98.
51 *Ibid.*, p. 98.
52 Quoted in *ibid.*, p. 32.
53 Said, *Orientalism*, p. 32.
54 Quoted in *ibid.*, pp. 32–3.
55 Quoted in *ibid.*, p. 34.
56 Said, *Orientalism*, p. 34.
57 Quoted in *ibid.*, p. 36.
58 Quoted in *ibid.*, p. 37.
59 Said, *Orientalism*, p. 38.
60 *Ibid.*, p. 38.
61 Quoted in *ibid.*, pp. 38–9.
62 Said, *Orientalism*, p. 40.
63 *Ibid.*, p. 43.
64 *Ibid.*, p. 44.
65 Karl Marx, *Surveys from Exile*, ed. David Fernbach (London: Pelican, 1973), pp. 306–7; quoted in Said, *Orientalism*, p. 153.
66 Said, *Orientalism*, p. 45.
67 Said, *The Question of Palestine* (1979; London: Vintage, 1992), p. 56.
68 *Ibid.*, pp. 56–7.
69 *Ibid.*, p. 57.
70 *Ibid.*, p. 57.
71 *Ibid.*, p. 57.
72 *Ibid.*, p. 59.
73 *Ibid.*, p. 60.
74 *Ibid.*, p. 60.
75 *Ibid.*, p. 61.
76 *Ibid.*, p. 61.
77 *Ibid.*, p. 65.
78 *Ibid.*, p. 66.

79 *Ibid.*, p. 66.
80 *Ibid.*, p. 68.
81 *Ibid.*, p. 69.
82 Quoted in *ibid.*, pp. 70–1.
83 Said, *The Question of Palestine*, p. 73.
84 *Ibid.*, pp. 73–4.
85 *Ibid.*, p. 74.
86 *Ibid.*, p. 81.
87 *Ibid.*, pp. 86–7.
88 *Ibid.*, p. 87.
89 *Ibid.*, pp. 96–7.
90 Said, *Orientalism*, p. 12.
91 Said, *The Question of Palestine*, p. 103.
92 *Ibid.*, p. 110.
93 Said, *The Politics of Dispossession: The Struggle for Palestinian Self-Determination 1969–1994* (London: Chatto and Windus, 1994), pp. 247–68.
94 Hayden White, *The Content of the Form: Narrative Discourse and Historical Representation* (Baltimore, MD: Johns Hopkins University Press, 1987), pp. 11–14.
95 Said, *The Politics of Dispossession*, p. 249.
96 *Ibid.*, p. 254.
97 *Ibid.*, p. 252.
98 *Ibid.*, p. 257.
99 Said, *The World, the Text, and the Critic*, p. 2; Benda (1867–1956) was a French philosopher. *La Trahison des Clercs* [The Betrayal of the Intellectuals], published in 1927, was an attack on contemporary French intellectuals whom he accused of having given up rationalistic intellectual independence, in favour of the promotion of aggressive nationalism.
100 Said, *The World, the Text, and the Critic*, p. 2.
101 *Ibid.*, p. 3.
102 *Ibid.*, p. 4.
103 *Ibid.*, p. 5.
104 Erich Auerbach, 'Philology and *Weltliteratur*', trans. M. and E. W. Said, *Centennial Review*, 13 (Winter 1969), p. 17; quoted in Said, *The World, the Text, and the Critic*, p. 7.
105 Said, *The World, the Text, and the Critic*, p. 8.
106 *Ibid.*, p. 9.
107 *Ibid.*, p. 10.
108 *Ibid.*, p. 10.
109 *Ibid.*, p. 10.
110 *Ibid.*, p. 11.
111 *Ibid.*, p. 11.
112 Quoted in *ibid.*, p. 12.
113 Said, *The World, the Text, and the Critic*, p. 16.

114 *Ibid.*, p. 24.
115 *Ibid.*, p. 28.
116 *Ibid.*, p. 28.
117 *Ibid.*, p. 27.
118 *Ibid.*, p. 82.
119 *Ibid.*, p. 87.
120 *Ibid.*, p. 28.
121 *Ibid.*, p. 144.
122 *Ibid.*, p. 145.
123 *Ibid.*, p. 148.
124 *Ibid.*, p. 183.
125 *Ibid.*, p. 212.
126 *Ibid.*, p. 215.
127 *Ibid.*, p. 221.
128 *Ibid.*, p. 221.
129 *Ibid.*, p. 221.
130 *Ibid.*, p. 222.
131 *Ibid.*, p. 242.
132 *Ibid.*, p. 245; Baruch Spinoza (1632–77) was a Dutch Jewish philosopher, who formulated a theory of the unity of God and Nature, and also of a fundamentalist determinism, where human freedom consisted only in the acknowledgment and embracing of necessity.
133 Said, *The World, the Text, and the Critic*, p. 26.
134 *Ibid.*, p. 53.
135 *Ibid.*, p. 29.
136 Said, *Culture and Imperialism* (London: Chatto and Windus, 1993), p. 19.
137 Conrad, *Heart of Darkness*, ed. Paul Armstrong (New York: W. W. Norton, 2006), p. 27.
138 Said, *Culture and Imperialism*, p. 25.
139 *Ibid.*, p. 32.
140 *Ibid.*, p. 36.
141 *Ibid.*, pp. 50–1.
142 *Ibid.*, p. 56.
143 *Ibid.*, p. 59.
144 *Ibid.*, pp. 59–60.
145 *Ibid.*, p. 75.
146 *Ibid.*, p. 82.
147 *Ibid.*, pp. 83–4.
148 *Ibid.*, pp. 85–6.
149 *Ibid.*, p. 91.
150 *Ibid.*, p. 83.
151 *Ibid.*, p. 93.
152 *Ibid.*, p. 93.

153 *Ibid.*, p. 101.
154 *Ibid.*, p. 104.
155 *Ibid.*, p. 106.
156 *Ibid.*, p. 107.
157 *Ibid.*, p. 115.
158 *Ibid.*, pp. 265–6.
159 *Ibid.*, pp. 271–2; see Alfred Crosby, *Ecological Imperialism: The Biological Expansion of Europe, 900–1900* (Cambridge: Cambridge University Press, 1986).
160 Said, *Culture and Imperialism*, p. 272; see Neil Smith, *Uneven Development: Nature, Capital and the Production of Space* (Oxford: Blackwell, 1984).
161 Said, *Culture and Imperialism*, pp. 274–5; see Seamus Deane, *Celtic Revivals: Essays in Modern Irish Literature 1880–1980* (London: Faber and Faber, 1985).
162 Conor Cruise O'Brien, 'Passion and Cunning: An Essay on the Politics of W. B. Yeats' in A. N. Jeffares and K. G. W Cross (eds.), *In Excited Reverie: A Centenary Tribute to William Butler Yeats 1865–1939* (London: Macmillan, 1965), pp. 207–78; see also Elizabeth Cullingford, *Yeats, Ireland and Fascism* (London: Macmillan, 1981).
163 Said, *Culture and Imperialism*, p. 276.
164 Fanon, *The Wretched of the Earth*, trans. Constance Farrington (London: Penguin, 1967), p. 170.
165 Said, *Culture and Imperialism*, p. 288.
166 *Ibid.*, p. 320.
167 Paul A. Bové, 'Hope and Reconcilation: A Review of Edward W. Said', *boundary 2*, 20:2 (1993), pp. 266–82.

4 Reception

1 Bernard Lewis, 'The Question of Orientalism', *New York Review of Books*, 29:11 (24 June 1982), pp. 49–56.
2 Edward Said and Bernard Lewis, 'Orientalism: An Exchange', *New York Review of Books*, 29:12 (12 August 1982), pp. 46–8.
3 James Clifford, *The Predicament of Culture: Twentieth-Century Ethnography, Literature, and Art* (Cambridge, MA: Harvard University Press, 1988), p. 256.
4 Clifford, *The Predicament of Culture*, p. 256.
5 *Ibid.*, p. 260.
6 *Ibid.*, p. 261.
7 Said, *Orientalism*, p. 197.
8 *Ibid.*, p. 272.
9 Clifford, *The Predicament of Culture*, p. 263.
10 *Ibid.*, p. 270.
11 *Ibid.*, p. 272.
12 *Ibid.*, p. 275.

13 Paul A. Bové, *Intellectuals in Power: A Genealogy of Critical Humanism* (New York: Columbia University Press, 1986), pp. 213–14.

14 Bové, *Intellectuals in Power*, p. 216.

15 *Ibid.*, p. 222.

16 *Ibid.*, p. 234.

17 Robert Young, *White Mythologies: Writing History and the West* (London: Routledge, 1990), p. 2.

18 Said, 'Orientalism Reconsidered' in his *Reflections on Exile and Other Essays* (Cambridge, MA: Harvard University Press, 2000), pp. 198–215 (pp. 209–10).

19 Young, *White Mythologies*, pp. 129–30.

20 *Ibid.*, p. 132.

21 *Ibid.*, p. 135.

22 Said, 'The Problem of Textuality: Two Exemplary Positions', *Critical Inquiry*, 4:4 (Summer 1978), pp. 673–714; Said, *The World, the Text, and the Critic*, pp. 178–225.

23 Young, *White Mythologies*, p. 139.

24 *Ibid.*, p. 139.

25 Aijaz Ahmad, '*Orientalism* and After: Ambivalence and Metropolitan Location in the Work of Edward Said' in his *In Theory: Classes, Nations, Literatures* (London: Verso, 1992), pp. 159–219 (p. 163).

26 Ahmad, '*Orientalism* and After', p. 164.

27 *Ibid.*, pp. 168–9.

28 Said, *Orientalism*, pp. 272, 273.

29 Ahmad, '*Orientalism* and After', pp. 193–4.

30 *Ibid.*, pp. 194–5.

31 *Ibid.*, p. 195.

32 *Ibid.*, pp. 194–5.

33 *Ibid.*, pp. 195–6.

34 *Ibid.*, p. 196.

35 Lata Mani and Ruth Frankenberg, 'The Challenge of *Orientalism*', *Economy and Society*, 14:2 (1985), pp. 174–92.

36 Joan Miller, *Seductions: Studies in Reading and Culture* (London: Virago, 1990).

37 Reina Lewis, *Gendering Orientalism: Race, Femininity and Representation* (New York: Routledge, 1995).

38 Said, 'Orientalism Reconsidered', p. 201.

39 *Ibid.*, p. 202.

40 *Ibid.*, p. 203.

41 *Ibid.*, p. 203.

42 *Ibid.*, p. 206.

43 *Ibid.*, pp. 211–12.

44 *Ibid.*, p. 214.

45 *Ibid.*, p. 215.

46 Said, *Representations of the Intellectual*, p. 13.

Guide to further reading

Works by Edward W. Said

Said, Edward W., *Joseph Conrad and the Fiction of Autobiography* (1966; New York: Columbia University Press, 2008)
    Beginnings: Intention and Method (1975; New York: Columbia University Press, 1985)
    Orientalism (1978; London: Penguin, 2003)
    The Question of Palestine (1979; London: Vintage, 1992)
    Covering Islam: How the Media and the Experts Determine How We See the Rest of the World (1981; London: Vintage, 1997)
    The World, the Text, and the Critic (London: Faber and Faber, 1983)
    After the Last Sky (London: Faber and Faber, 1986)
    Musical Elaborations (London: Chatto and Windus, 1991)
    Culture and Imperialism (London: Chatto and Windus, 1993)
    The Politics of Dispossession: The Struggle for Palestinian Self-Determination 1969–1994 (London: Chatto and Windus, 1994)
    Representations of the Intellectual: The 1993 Reith Lectures (New York: Pantheon, 1994)
    Peace and Its Discontents: Gaza–Jericho 1993–1995 (London: Vintage, 1995)
    Out of Place: A Memoir (London: Granta, 1999)
    The End of the Peace Process: Oslo and After (London: Granta, 2000)
    Reflections on Exile and Other Essays (Cambridge, MA: Harvard University Press, 2000)
    Power, Politics, and Culture: Interviews with Edward W. Said, ed. and intro. Gauri Viswanathan (New York: Pantheon, 2001)
    Freud and the Non-European (London: Verso, 2003)
    From Oslo to Iraq and the Roadmap (London: Bloomsbury, 2004)
    Humanism and Democratic Criticism (New York: Columbia University Press, 2004)
    On Late Style (London: Bloomsbury, 2006)
    Music at the Limits (New York: Columbia University Press, 2008)
Said, Edward and Daniel Barenboim, *Parallels and Paradoxes: Explorations in Music and Society*, ed. Ara Guzelimian (New York: Pantheon, 2002)

Said, Edward and Christopher Hitchens (eds.), *Blaming the Victims: Spurious Scholarship and the Palestine Question* (London: Verso, 1988)

Recommended reading

Ahmad, Aijaz, *In Theory: Classes, Nations, Literatures* (London: Verso, 1992)
Ansell-Pearson, Keith, Benita Parry, and Judith Squires (eds.), *Cultural Readings of Imperialism: Edward Said and the Gravity of History* (London: Lawrence and Wishart, 1997)
Aruri, Naseer and Muhammad A. Shuraydi (eds.), *Revising Culture, Reinventing Peace: The Influence of Edward W. Said* (New York: Olive Branch Press, 2001)
Ashcroft, Bill and Pal Ahluwalia, *Edward Said* (London: Routledge, 2008)
Bové, Paul A., *Intellectuals in Power: A Genealogy of Critical Humanism* (New York: Columbia University Press, 1986)
Bové, Paul A. (ed.), *Edward Said and the Work of the Critic: Speaking Truth to Power* (Durham, NC: Duke University Press, 2000)
Brennan, Tim, *Wars of Position: The Cultural Politics of Left and Right* (New York: Columbia University Press, 2006)
Clifford, James, *The Predicament of Culture: Twentieth-Century Ethnography, Literature, and Art* (Cambridge, MA: Harvard University Press, 1988)
Deane, Seamus, 'Under Eastern and Western Eyes', *boundary 2*, 28:1 (Spring 2001), pp. 1–18
    'Edward Said (1935–2003): A Late Style of Humanism', *The Field Day Review*, 1 (2004), pp. 189–202
Hart, William D., *Edward Said and the Religious Effects of Culture* (Cambridge: Cambridge University Press, 2000)
Hussein, Abdirahman A., *Edward Said: Criticism and Society* (London: Verso, 2002)
Nagy-Zekmi, Silvia (ed.), *Paradoxical Citizenship: Edward Said* (Lanham, MD: Lexington Books, 2006)
Radhakrishnan, R., *History, the Human, and the World Between* (Durham, NC: Duke University Press, 2008)
Singh, Amritjit and Bruce G. Johnson (eds.), *Interviews with Edward W. Said* (Jackson, MI: University Press of Mississippi, 2004)
Sokmen, Muge and Basak Ertur (eds.), *Waiting for the Barbarians: A Tribute to Edward Said* (London: Verso, 2008)
Spanos, William, *The Legacy of Edward W. Said* (Chicago: University of Illinois Press, 2009)
Sprinker, Michael (ed.), *Edward Said: A Critical Reader* (Oxford: Blackwell, 1992)
Varadharajan, Asha, *Exotic Parodies: Subjectivity in Adorno, Said, and Spivak* (Minneapolis, MN: University of Minnesota Press, 1995)
Williams, Patrick (ed.), *Edward Said*, Sage Masters in Modern Social Thought, 4 vols. (London: Sage Books, 2001)

Periodicals: special issues on Edward Said

Alif: Journal of Comparative Poetics, 25 (2005) – 'Edward Said and Critical
        Decolonization'
boundary 2: an international journal of literature and culture, 25:2 (Summer
        1998) – 'Edward Said'
boundary 2: an international journal of literature and culture, 31:2 (Summer
        2004) – 'Critical Secularism'
Critical Inquiry, 31:2 (Winter 2005) – 'Edward Said: Continuing the
        Conversation'
Diacritics, 6:3 (Fall 1976)
Journal of Palestine Studies, 33:3 (Spring 2004) – 'Special Issue in Honor of
        Edward W. Said'
Social Text, 24:2 (Summer 2006) – 'Edward Said: A Memorial Issue'

Index

Cambridge Introductions to . . .

AUTHORS

Jane Austen Janet Todd

Samuel Beckett Ronan McDonald

Walter Benjamin David Ferris

J. M. Coetzee Dominic Head

Joseph Conrad John Peters

Jacques Derrida Leslie Hill

Emily Dickinson Wendy Martin

George Eliot Nancy Henry

T. S. Eliot John Xiros Cooper

William Faulkner Theresa M. Towner

F. Scott Fitzgerald Kirk Curnutt

Michel Foucault Lisa Downing

Robert Frost Robert Faggen

Nathaniel Hawthorne Leland S. Person

Zora Neale Hurston Lovalerie King

James Joyce Eric Bulson

Herman Melville Kevin J. Hayes

Sylvia Plath Jo Gill

Edgar Allen Poe Benjamin F. Fisher

Ezra Pound Ira Nadel

Jean Rhys Elaine Savory

Edward Said Conor McCarthy

Shakespeare Emma Smith

Shakespeare's Comedies Penny Gay

Shakespeare's History Plays Warren Chernaik

Shakespeare's Tragedies Janette Dillon

Harriet Beecher Stowe Sarah Robbins

Mark Twain Peter Messent

Virginia Woolf Jane Goldman

W. B. Yeats David Holdeman

Edith Wharton Pamela Knights

Walt Whitman M. Jimmie Killingsworth

TOPICS

The American Short Story Martin Scofield

Comedy Eric Weitz

Creative Writing David Morley

Early English Theatre Janette Dillon

English Theatre, 1660–1900 Peter Thomson

Francophone Literature Patrick Corcoran

Modern British Theatre Simon Shepherd

Modern Irish Poetry Justin Quinn

Modernism Pericles Lewis

Narrative (second edition) H. Porter Abbott

The Nineteenth-Century American Novel Gregg Crane

Postcolonial Literatures C. L. Innes

Postmodern Fiction Bran Nicol

Russian Literature Caryl Emerson

Scenography Joslin McKinney and Philip Butterworth

The Short Story in English Adrian Hunter

Theatre Historiography Thomas Postlewait

Theatre Studies Christopher Balme

Tragedy Jennifer Wallace

Printed in the United States
By Bookmasters